W9-CED-066

World Civilizations and Cultures

Author: Don Blattner

Editors: Mary Dieterich and Sarah M. Anderson

Proofreader: Margaret Brown

COPYRIGHT © 2012 Mark Twain Media, Inc.

ISBN 978-1-58037-634-1

Printing No. CD-404159

Mark Twain Media, Inc., Publishers
Distributed by Carson-Dellosa Publishing LLC

Table of Contents

Introduction to the Teacher

World Civilizations and Cultures follows the development of civilizations from their primitive beginnings in the Fertile Crescent over 5,000 years ago to more recent civilizations in Europe, Asia, and the Americas. It will not only examine many important civilizations and describe them in detail, but it will also highlight the achievements each civilization has contributed to our present life.

This book will also point out how cultures borrowed from previous cultures. This refining process, repeated many times, has given us the world we live in today. It must be emphasized that when studying one civilization or culture at a time, students should be reminded that other civilizations and cultures were thriving simultaneously. One civilization did not abruptly end and another dramatically begin. For example, while the Assyrians were thriving, so were the Etruscans, Greeks, Phoenicians, and others.

This book is part of the *Civilizations of the Past* series from Mark Twain Media, Inc. It is specifically designed to facilitate planning for the diverse learning styles and skills levels of middle-school students. The special features of the book provide the teacher with alternative methods of instruction. A modified version of the text is available for download for struggling readers.

Book Features:
- **<u>Reading Selection</u>** introduces facts and information as a reading exercise.
- **<u>Knowledge Check</u>** assesses student understanding of the reading exercise using selected response and constructed response questioning strategies.
- **<u>Map Follow-Up</u>** provides opportunities for students to report information from a spatial perspective.
- **<u>Explore</u>** allows students to expand learning by participating in high-interest, hands-on and research activities.

Online Resources:
Reluctant Reader Text: A modified version of the reading exercise pages can be downloaded from the website at www.carsondellosa.com. In the Search box, enter the product code CD-404159. When you reach the *World Civilizations and Cultures* product page, click the Resources or Downloads tab. Then click on the Lower Reading Level Text Download.

The readability level of the text has been modified to facilitate struggling readers. The Flesch-Kincaid Readability formula, which is built into Microsoft® Word™, was used to determine the readability level. The formula calculates the number of words, syllables, and sentences in each paragraph, producing a reading level.

Additional Resources:
Classroom decoratives appeal to visual learners. The *Ancient Civilizations and Cultures Topper; Greek and Roman Civilizations*; and *Mayan, Incan, and Aztec* Bulletin Board Sets, available from Mark Twain Media, Inc., can be used to visually reinforce lessons found in this book in an interesting and attention-grabbing way. The *Eastern Hemisphere Maps* or *World Geography: Middle-East Maps* Bulletin Board Sets are also helpful when studying the geography of the European, Asian, and African civilizations.

The Fertile Crescent

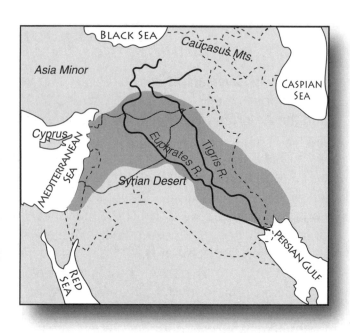

Fertile Crescent

The term "**Fertile Crescent**" refers to an area in the Middle East where the earliest known civilizations of the world began. The area got its name because the soil is fertile, or rich, and the region is shaped like a crescent. Like a huge arch, the Fertile Crescent covers an area from the Persian Gulf through the Tigris and Euphrates River valleys and along the Mediterranean Sea. Some people refer to the eastern part of the Fertile Crescent as Mesopotamia. The western part of the Fertile Crescent is sometimes referred to as the Mediterranean section.

Nomads Settle in the Fertile Crescent

The Fertile Crescent was an ideal place for **nomadic** people to settle, build cities, and eventually develop civilizations. Sheep, goats, and various kinds of grains were found in abundance in the wild. With a permanent food source, there was no need to move around to find food. It was easier to grow crops in the rich soil and to raise animals for food. People living in the Fertile Crescent were able to grow more crops than they could eat and raise more animals than they needed, so they could **trade** the excess crops and animals with others. As trading increased, the population grew, and the people needed to develop laws, keep records, and invent ways to deal with their new way of life. There was a need for a written language, mathematics, laws, medicine, **agriculture**, and other developments because of the many people living close to one another.

The First Civilizations Develop

When humans changed their lifestyle from hunters and fishers to farmers about 5,000 years ago in the Fertile Crescent, the developments and inventions that came from this change helped to develop the world's first **civilizations**. These civilizations have affected world history tremendously, not only in social and business areas, but in religion as well. Many of the great religions that exist in the world today had their beginnings in the area known as the Fertile Crescent.

Later Civilizations

The Fertile Crescent was not only the home of the first civilizations, but also the area where many later civilizations were developed. Some of the civilizations that developed in the Fertile Crescent were the Assyrians, Sumerians, Canaanites, Philistines, Phoenicians/Carthaginians, Akkadians, Hittites, Babylonians, Egyptians, Israelites, and others.

Name: _____ Date: _____

Knowledge Check

Matching

_____ 1. Fertile Crescent

_____ 2. nomadic

_____ 3. trade

_____ 4. agriculture

_____ 5. civilization

a. farming; growing crops and raising livestock

b. moving from place to place with no permanent home

c. an arch-shaped area in the Middle East from the Persian Gulf through the Tigris and Euphrates River Valleys and along the Mediterranean Sea

d. a high level of cultural and technological development, especially when systems of writing and record-keeping have been created

e. exchanging goods or services with other people

Multiple Choice

6. The eastern part of the Fertile Crescent is sometimes called
   a. the Mediterranean.
   b. Mesopotamia.
   c. Asia Minor.
   d. Egypt.

7. What was one food source that was NOT available to the nomadic people in the Fertile Crescent?
   a. sheep
   b. grains
   c. potatoes
   d. goats

8. Why were people able to begin trading with others in the area?
   a. They had extra food.
   b. They ate everything they grew.
   c. They spent all their time farming.
   d. They lived close to one another.

9. Which civilization was NOT developed in the Fertile Crescent?
   a. Sumerians
   b. Israelites
   c. Minoans
   d. Akkadians

Constructed Response

10. What parts of a civilization developed as people in the Fertile Crescent began to grow more crops and raise more animals than they needed for themselves? Use details from the reading selection to help support your answer.

_____

_____

_____

_____

_____

_____

Name: _____ Date: _____

Map Follow-Up:
Identifying Modern Countries in the Fertile Crescent

Using an atlas, identify the modern Middle-Eastern countries that exist in the areas in and around the Fertile Crescent on the map below. The outlines of the countries are shown as dashed lines.

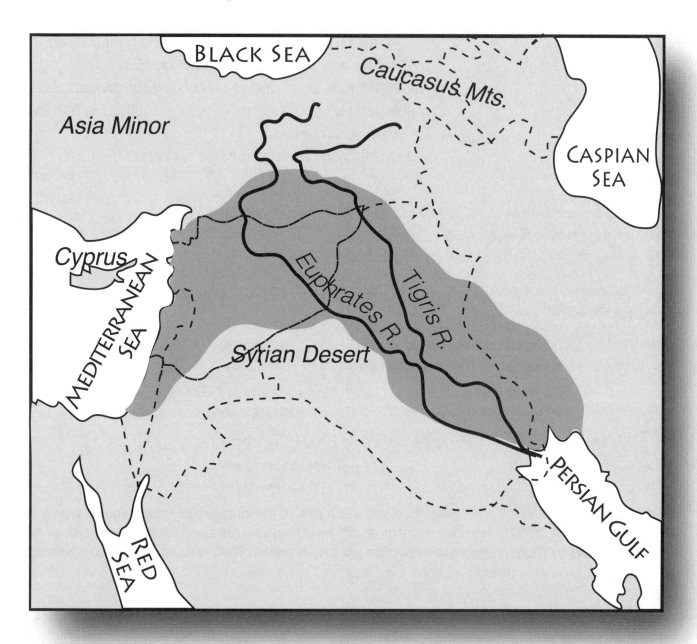

Mesopotamia

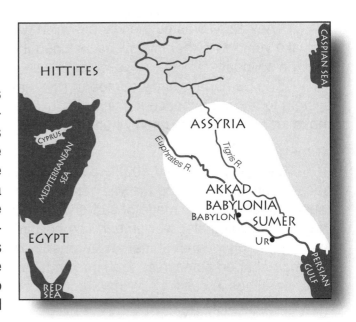

The Land Between Two Rivers

Mesopotamia is a Greek word that means "between two rivers." The two rivers are the Tigris and Euphrates Rivers. They begin in what is now Turkey, flow southeast, come together in the southeast in what is now Iraq, and empty into the Persian Gulf. The hot, dry climate of Mesopotamia was mixed with seasonal flooding, which made farming a challenge. Farmers in ancient Mesopotamia learned to build levees to control the floods and develop irrigation systems in order to produce wheat, barley, sesame, and flax. They were also able to produce many different kinds of fruits and vegetables.

Mesopotamia was actually an area, not a civilization. It was composed of several independent city-states, each with its own religion, laws, language, and government. Many civilizations have existed in Mesopotamia, some of them at the same time. Some of the cultures that have existed in this area are Sumeria, Assyria, Babylon, and Iraq.

The Sumerians

The first group of people to inhabit Mesopotamia were the **Sumerians**. They originally lived in the mountains but moved to the Plain of Shinar near the Persian Gulf to take advantage of the fertile soil. First, they drained the marshes and then controlled the Tigris and Euphrates

---

SUMERIAN CIVILIZATION AT A GLANCE

WHERE: In the Middle East, between the Tigris and Euphrates Rivers

WHEN: 3500 B.C.–2000 B.C.

ACHIEVEMENTS:

- The world's first civilization where people lived together in a city-state
- Invented a written language
- Developed science and mathematics to a high degree; were able to divide the year and the circle into 360 parts
- Developed a twelve-month calendar based on lunar cycles
- Used the wheel and made vehicles
- Invented the plow and the sailboat

Rivers by building levees and irrigation canals. As a result, the Sumerians had a stable food supply, and not everyone was needed to farm, hunt, or fish. Some Sumerians became tradesmen, merchants, soldiers, priests, government officials, and artisans. Their country was called **Sumer**.

Cuneiform Written on a Clay Tablet

Sumerian Inventions

The Sumerians are given credit for many inventions. One of the most important was the invention of a written language. Writing was invented so the Sumerians could keep records. Their writing was very simple. It was composed of pictures called **pictographs**. **Scribes**, who were professional writers, drew the pictures on clay tablets using a wedge-shaped instrument, or **stylus**. Over a period of time, the writing became more sophisticated. The pictures were replaced with shapes and lines. This type of writing is called **cuneiform**.

They also invented the wheel, which was developed for making pottery, but was later used to make vehicles. Other inventions included the water clock, the twelve-month calendar, the plow, and the sailboat.

The Sumerians had a numbering system based on the number 60. We still use the Sumerian system today when measuring time. For example, sixty seconds make a minute and sixty minutes make an hour. It is also used when measuring a circle with 360 degrees.

Sumerian Cities

Between 3500 and 2000 B.C., the Sumerians were living in large villages. Eventually they became prosperous, and the villages developed into self-governing city-states. The buildings in these city-states were made of sun-dried mud bricks. There was plenty of mud from the rivers but very little building stone or timber. The buildings in Sumer were different from other civilizations, such as the Egyptians. Sumerians learned how to use a keystone to make arches. A **keystone** is a wedge-shaped stone in an arch that causes the arch to lock together. The doorways, gates, and other openings in buildings in the Sumerian cities had arches. Similar openings in Egyptian buildings were square.

Sumerian Religion

Religion was important to the Sumerians. At the center of each city-state was a temple that was surrounded by courts and public buildings. These temples were called **ziggurats**. Ziggurats eventually became temple-towers brightly decorated with glazed bricks. They were like huge pyramids with terraced sides that were flat on the top.

This ancient ziggurat in present-day Iraq has been reconstructed.

The Sumerians had many gods. They believed the gods spoke to them through their priests. The priests had a great deal of power in Sumer. When a priest commanded that something be done, the people believed the command was actually coming from one of their gods, and they obeyed. The priests eventually became priest-kings and ruled large areas.

Dealing With Invaders

The great disadvantage in Mesopotamia was that the land did not provide any natural protection from invaders. Enemies could easily march into Sumer from almost any direction. This made Sumerians vulnerable to attack, not only from foreign armies, but from other Sumerian cities as well. Wars between Sumerian cities were common.

The Akkadians

The **Akkadians** moved into Sumeria from the Arabian Peninsula. They were a Semitic people. This means they spoke a **Semitic** language related to Arabic and Hebrew. The Akkadians formed their own country where the Tigris and the Euphrates Rivers were close together. Their country was called **Akkad**. The Akkadians adopted much of the Sumerian culture. After many clashes, more Semites invaded Sumeria. The Sumerian culture was eventually absorbed by the invaders. This combined civilization lasted until about 1950 B.C. when the Amorites and the Elamites captured Ur, Mesopotamia's most important city.

Name: _____ Date: _____

Knowledge Check

Matching

_____ 1. Mesopotamia

_____ 2. pictographs

_____ 3. scribes

_____ 4. stylus

_____ 5. cuneiform

_____ 6. keystone

_____ 7. ziggurat

_____ 8. Semitic

a. a wedge-shaped instrument for writing

b. temple-tower that was the center of Sumerian cities

c. writing consisting of shapes and lines produced by using a wedge-shaped instrument on a clay tablet

d. the land between the Tigris and Euphrates Rivers

e. a language related to Arabic and Hebrew

f. a wedge-shaped stone in an arch that causes the arch to lock together

g. professional writers

h. pictures that stand for words

Multiple Choice

9. The first group of people to live in Mesopotamia were the _____.

   a. Akkadians

   b. Sumerians

   c. Babylonians

   d. Assyrians

10. These people in Sumeria eventually became so powerful that they became kings and ruled large areas.

   a. priests

   b. farmers

   c. scribes

   d. soldiers

11. The Sumerian numbering system that is still used today is based on the number _____.

   a. 5

   b. 10

   c. 30

   d. 60

Constructed Response

12. What were some of the advantages and disadvantages of living in Mesopotamia? Use details from the reading selection to support your answer.

_____

_____

_____

_____

_____

_____

Babylonia

Reconstruction of the Gate of Ishtar

The Rise of Babylonia

One Akkadian town that developed in approximately 1900 B.C. was the small town of Babylon, located by the Euphrates River. Babylon grew in size and importance, and eventually its ruler, King Hammurabi, conquered all of Mesopotamia. This kingdom came to be known as **Babylonia**.

The Babylonian culture was similar to the Sumerian culture, which had existed in Mesopotamia before the Babylonians arrived. In fact, many people refer to the Babylonians as just a later development of the Sumerian culture. While the two civilizations existed at different times, they had many things in common. The Babylonians adopted the religion, literature, inventions, and practices of the Sumerians. Scholars and priests spoke the Sumerian language, although most Babylonians did not. Babylonia did make one important contribution of its own to the world. This contribution was a code of laws known as the ***Code of Hammurabi***.

The Code of Hammurabi

Hammurabi was king of Babylonia from 1792 to 1750 B.C. He was a powerful leader with strong armies. He expanded Babylon by conquering other kingdoms. Hammurabi was also an efficient administrator. Hammurabi was not just concerned with his own comfort. He was also concerned with the lives of *all* of the people in his kingdom. He wanted everyone in his kingdom to have enough food, adequate housing, and to be treated fairly. In order to make sure that everyone was treated fairly, he had his scribes draw up a code of laws that are known as the *Code of Hammurabi*. Many of the laws were borrowed from the written laws of the Sumerians. Hammurabi's code was a little different from the laws devised by the Sumerians, however. Hammurabi's code added the element of revenge. In Sumeria, most who committed a crime were fined. The *Code of Hammurabi* did not impose a fine on criminals, but substituted the ancient punishment of *"an eye for an eye, and a tooth for a tooth."* In other words, if someone did something bad to a person, in many cases, the court would do the same thing to the wrongdoer.

The Code of Hammurabi engraved on a stele.

BABYLONIAN CIVILIZATION AT A GLANCE

WHERE: On the Euphrates River
WHEN: 2000–1155 B.C.
ACHIEVEMENTS:
- Devised a code of laws, known as the *Code of Hammurabi*, designed to protect the weak
- Studied astronomy
- Built beautiful buildings as well as the Gate of Ishtar and the Hanging Gardens of Babylon

---

Some laws in the code seem very extreme and cruel. For example, if a son slapped his father, the son's hands would be cut off. If a man killed another man's son, then his son would be killed. While this may seem harsh by today's standards, before the code was written and followed, punishment was often decided by priests and judges who imposed punishments even more harsh. Death was a common punishment for even the most minor offenses. So these laws were not meant to be cruel, but to be fair.

The Code did distinguish between classes of people. A person's punishment depended on who was wronged. For example, if a man put out the eye of another man, his eye would then be put out. But if he put out the eye of a freed man (a former slave), he would pay one gold mina. If he put out the eye of a man's slave, he would then have to pay one-half of the slave's value.

Astronomy

Law was not the only interest of the Babylonians. They studied astronomy and also believed in astrology. **Astronomy** is the study of the universe, including the movement of the stars and planets. **Astrology** is the belief that the positions and movements of the planets and stars can affect or predict life on Earth. While we separate these two areas today, the Babylonians did not.

The Babylonians not only watched the stars and heavens, they kept records of events, such as when an eclipse occurred. They were able to measure time by studying the movements of the celestial bodies. The priests used their knowledge of planets and the stars as part of their religion. The priests claimed that by studying the celestial bodies, they could tell the future. They were constantly looking at the skies, making horoscopes and predictions based on what they saw. A **horoscope** is a prediction of a person's future based on a diagram of the planets and stars at a given moment, such as birth.

Nebuchadnezzar II

About 1,000 years after the death of Hammurabi, King Nebuchadnezzar II came to power. By this time, Babylon was part of the Chaldean Empire, which came to power after the Assyrian Empire was destroyed. Nebuchadnezzar ruled Babylon from 605 to 562 B.C., and under his leadership, Babylon grew. At this time, Babylon had two structures that were so impressive they were known throughout the civilized world. The first was the beautifully decorated wall surrounding Babylon. On top of the wall were towers for guards who could watch for approaching enemies. This wall was wide enough for a four-horse chariot to be driven on it. The most impressive gate in the wall was the **Gate of Ishtar**. Ishtar was a goddess, and the gate named in her honor was made of colorful glazed enamel bricks with pictures of animals. The gate was so beautiful that at one time it was considered as one of the Seven Wonders of the Ancient World. It was later replaced on the list by the Lighthouse at Alexandria.

The second structure built by Nebuchadnezzar to gain worldwide fame was the **Hanging Gardens of Babylon**. The Hanging Gardens is still considered one of the Seven Wonders of the Ancient World. It was built to please Nebuchadnezzar's wife, Amytis. It was a building consisting of several terraces, one above the other. Each terrace was planted with trees and flowers from around the country. Pools and fountains were also built into the structure. The Babylonians developed an irrigation system to raise water from the Euphrates River to the Gardens. Exactly how this irrigation system worked is unknown, but later writers referred to the system as "water engines."

The Hanging Gardens of Babylon

Nebuchadnezzar was succeeded by his son in 562 B.C. who was assassinated three years later. Within a few years, Babylon was invaded by the Persians, and Babylon became part of the Persian Empire.

Name: _____ Date: _____

Knowledge Check

Matching

_____ 1. Babylonia

_____ 2. Code of Hammurabi

_____ 3. astronomy

_____ 4. astrology

_____ 5. horoscope

_____ 6. Gate of Ishtar

_____ 7. Hanging Gardens
        of Babylon

a. the belief that the positions and movements of the stars and planets can affect or predict life on Earth

b. a prediction of a person's future based on a diagram of the stars and planets at a given moment

c. the study of the universe, including the movement of the stars and planets

d. the most impressive opening in the wall around Babylon; named in honor of a goddess

e. a set of laws and punishments developed by the king of Babylonia

f. kingdom that covered all of Mesopotamia, ruled by King Hammurabi

g. building with irrigated terraces planted with trees and flowers and having pools and fountains; one of the Seven Wonders of the Ancient World

Multiple Choice

8. From where did the Babylonians adopt most of their culture?

   a. the Sumerians

   c. their own ideas

   b. the Egyptians

   d. the Persians

9. A man put out the eye of another man. The punishment depended on the class of the victim. For which class of victim was the punishment one gold mina?

   a. a slave

   c. a freed man

   b. a man of equal rank

   d. a servant

Constructed Response

10. How was the Code of Hammurabi attempting to be fair? Use details from the reading selection to help support your answer.

_____

_____

_____

_____

_____

_____

_____

The Assyrians

Assyria was a civilization in Mesopotamia on the upper Tigris River. The civilization lasted many centuries but was greatest between 1600 and 612 B.C. The Assyrians were a Semitic-speaking people who arrived in Mesopotamia about 2000 B.C. Assyria was named after its original capital, **Ashur**. Ashur gained its independence in about 1365 B.C.

Assyrian Advantages and Disadvantages

Assyria had several advantages over Babylonia. Assyrians could farm without the elaborate irrigation that was needed in Babylonia. The land received water from the Tigris River and its tributaries, and it also got a moderate amount of rainfall annually. Also, Assyria had rocks and stones that could be used for building. Assyria had two disadvantages, however. The Assyrian land was harder to cultivate, and they were often attacked by barbarians who raided their villages.

An Assyrian Lamassu

Assyrians developed a thriving trade in Anatolia (Asia Minor). Eventually, the Hittites drove the Assyrians out of Anatolia. During the time of the Babylonian Kingdom, Assyrian power in Mesopotamia grew weaker. By 1550 B.C., Assyria was part of the Mitanni Kingdom. The notable achievement of the **Mitanni Kingdom** was that it introduced trained horses and chariots into this part of the world.

The Assyrian Army

Gradually, Assyrian power grew and expanded by 1100 B.C. The Assyrians developed a **standing army**, which is composed of soldiers who choose the army as their career. When the soldiers are not fighting, they are still in the army, training to fight. This was a new idea in this period. Other countries fought their wars with citizen-soldiers. A **citizen-soldier** fights a war, and after it is over, he returns home and resumes his life working at his former craft or career. The Assyrian soldiers were fierce and cruel warriors. They had weapons made of iron rather than copper or bronze. They also had battering rams. They not only had foot soldiers, they had archers, chariots, and a cavalry. Whenever they captured enemies, they would either murder them or make them slaves.

The Assyrian Kingdom

Captured cities were plundered and looted. Citizens of conquered cities were required to pay taxes and **tribute** to the Assyrians. The Assyrians built forts close to these cities, and a governor was appointed for each fort. The governor reported directly to the king by sending reports by messengers on horseback—the first mail delivery service.

However, the kingdom became too large to maintain. There were too few soldiers, so mercenaries were hired to serve in the army. A **mercenary** is a foreign soldier hired by another country to fight in its army. Eventually, the Assyrians were vanquished by the Medes, Chaldeans, and the Babylonians. The capital city of **Nineveh** was razed.

ASSYRIAN CIVILIZATION AT A GLANCE

WHERE: Northern Mesopotamia
WHEN: 1600 B.C.–612 B.C.
ACHIEVEMENTS:
- Created the first library
- Built a system of roads
- Ruled their extended kingdom with appointed governors
- First to develop a standing army
- Developed a mail service

Name: _____ Date: _____

Knowledge Check

Matching

_____ 1. Mitanni Kingdom

_____ 2. standing army

_____ 3. citizen-soldier

_____ 4. tribute

_____ 5. mercenary

a. a foreign soldier hired by another country to fight in its army

b. a soldier who returns home and resumes his life when the fighting is over

c. composed of soldiers who choose the army as a career; when they are not fighting, they are training

d. introduced trained horses and chariots to the Mesopotamian region

e. payment that conquered people were required to pay to the conquerors

Multiple Choice

6. What was the name of Assyria's original capital?

    a. Nineveh   b. Babylon

    c. Ur   d. Ashur

7. How did the governors send reports to the king?

    a. carrier pigeons   b. messengers on horseback

    c. smoke signals   d. messages floated down river

8. Of what material were the Assyrians' weapons made?

    a. iron   b. stone

    c. bronze   d. copper

Constructed Response

9. Compare the Assyrian lands with Babylonia. Use details from the reading selection to help support your answer.

    _____

    _____

    _____

    _____

    _____

    _____

    _____

The Hittites

The **Hittites** were originally migrant peasants who lived north of the Black Sea. About 2300 B.C. they moved into **Anatolia**, which is the ancient name for Asia Minor. It is known as Turkey today. The land was rocky, but they could grow grain and graze animals. The land also held many metal ores.

Hittite City-States Become an Empire

The Hittite Civilization began in 1750 B.C. and lasted until 1200 B.C. It was not as organized as some other civilizations. The city-states that comprised the empire were spread throughout Asia Minor and Syria. They were often separated by mountains. Many city-states maintained their own languages and religions. The city-states often fought among themselves until Labarnas became king. Under his leadership, the Hittite empire grew to include most of Turkey. His son, Hattusilis I, expanded the empire into Syria. Hattusilis made the city of **Hattusa** the capital of the Hittite Kingdom. For protection, Hattusa was built high in the mountains and was protected by a stone wall 26 feet thick. Hattusilis' grandson, Mursilis, invaded and defeated Babylon. The crowds cheered and celebrated his great victory, but when he entered his palace, he was assassinated by his brother-in-law.

The Hittite and Egyptian treaty

Iron

The Hittite Civilization borrowed many ideas from other cultures. However, the Hittites did make two great contributions to humankind. The first was the use of iron. Weapons and tools had been made from copper or bronze, which are soft and bend easily. Iron is much harder. However, extracting the metal for use is more complicated than it is for other metals. The process of extracting ore is called **smelting**. Exactly when and where iron was first smelted is a mystery, but it is generally agreed that real iron **metallurgy** began with the Hittites some time between 1900 and 1400 B.C.

The First Treaty

The second notable accomplishment of the Hittite Empire, occurring in the 1200s B.C., was a treaty. The Hittites and the Egyptians decided that fighting each other was costly and inefficient. They signed a treaty pledging not to fight each other. If one was attacked by someone else, the other pledged to come to its defense. The treaty was engraved on a silver plaque, clay copies were placed in the Hittite library, and the Egyptians etched the treaty on walls. This was the first recorded treaty by two great powers.

Fair Laws

The Hittite laws were considered the fairest of the time. The Hittite law tried to **compensate** the person who was wronged. According to Babylonian law, if a man injured another, the man who caused the injury would be injured the same way. In the Hittite civilization, however, he would have to pay a fine to the person he injured.

HITTITE CIVILIZATION AT A GLANCE

WHERE: Anatolia, the ancient name for Asia Minor

WHEN: 1750 B.C.–1200 B.C.

ACHIEVEMENTS:
- One of the first civilizations to use iron
- Signed peace treaties
- Established a set of laws considered the fairest of the time

---

Name: _____ Date: _____

Knowledge Check

Matching

_____ 1. Hittites

_____ 2. Anatolia

_____ 3. Hattusa

_____ 4. smelting

_____ 5. metallurgy

_____ 6. compensate

a. the ancient name for Asia Minor; known as Turkey today

b. the science and technology of metals

c. migrant peasants who lived north of the Black Sea and then moved into Anatolia

d. pay back an equal amount for an injury or loss

e. the capital of the Hittite Kingdom

f. the process of extracting metal from ore

Multiple Choice

7. What was one of the Hittite Civilization's great gifts to humankind?
   a. defeating Babylon
   b. requiring injured people to be paid
   c. learning how to smelt iron ore
   d. uniting the Hittite city-states

8. Who united the Hittite city-states into an empire that included most of present-day Turkey?
   a. Hattusilis I
   b. Labarnas
   c. Mursilis
   d. Hammurabi

9. The first recorded treaty between two great powers involved what empires?
   a. Egypt and Sumeria
   b. the Hittites and Babylonia
   c. Assyria and Babylonia
   d. Egypt and the Hittites

Constructed Response

10. Why was the Hittite law code seen as the fairest of its time? Use details from the reading selection to help support your answer.

_____

_____

_____

_____

_____

_____

_____

_____

Ancient Egypt

The Great Pyramid of Giza and the Sphinx

Civilization Beside the Nile River

Each year between July and October, the **Nile River** floods and spills over its banks in the **Delta Region** before it empties into the Mediterranean Sea. This leaves behind a layer of **silt**, rich in nutrients that make it possible to grow crops in this otherwise arid land.

This is the fertile land that people began to settle in 3300 B.C. Drawn by the abundance of food provided by the Nile, people began to settle, farm, and build cities. This became the Egyptian Civilization. The Egyptians called their country the **Black Land**, referring to the fertile soil. The desert surrounding their country was referred to as the **Red Land**. The Red Land provided a natural barrier that protected Egypt from invaders. This is one of the reasons that the Egyptian civilization lasted over 3,000 years. It was the longest-lasting civilization in history.

Writing and Paper

Egyptian influence on other ancient civilizations has been considerable. Its writing system, called **hieroglyphics**, and other cultural elements were widely adapted by other ancient cultures. In addition to writing, the Egyptians developed a paper-like material from **papyrus** reed. They also used papyrus to make mats, ropes, toys, boats, and other items.

Building Skills

Egyptians were excellent architects, builders, craftsmen, and artisans. They built huge pyramids in which to bury their pharaohs. The **Great Pyramid of Giza** was so large and magnificent it was listed as one of the Seven Wonders of the Ancient World. It is the only one of these wonders that still stands today. The Great Pyramid was built over 5,000 years ago without modern machines or tools. Over 2.3 million stone blocks, each weighing about 2.5 tons, were transported from a stone quarry on the other side of the Nile and built into a pyramid about as high as a 42-story skyscraper. All of this was done with manpower alone. Also built near the Great Pyramid of Giza was the **Sphinx**, a huge stone sculpture of a creature with the face of a human and the body of a lion.

The Egyptians were superb engineers as well. They built canals, dams, and a reservoir to control the flood waters of the Nile. They even built a canal from the Nile to the Red Sea in order to improve trade.

Treatment of the Dead

Egyptians believed in life after death; a person's soul would continue to live as long as the body was preserved. The Egyptians practiced **mummification** of the dead. When someone died, their body was prepared in such a way that it would dry out and not decay. The bodies of the wealthy were wrapped in linen with jewels and protective charms inserted in the layers. The poor were often buried naked in shallow graves.

EGYPTIAN CIVILIZATION AT A GLANCE

WHERE: Along the Nile River in northeast Africa

WHEN: 3100 B.C.–332 B.C.

ACHIEVEMENTS:
- Built the pyramids, the sphinx, canals, and temples
- Invented a calendar with 365 days
- Made a paper-like material from the papyrus plant
- Used a loom to weave cloth
- Invented a system of writing called hieroglyphics

Name: _____ Date: _____

Knowledge Check

Matching

_____ 1. Delta Region

_____ 2. silt

_____ 3. Black Land

_____ 4. Red Land

_____ 5. heiroglyphics

_____ 6. papyrus

_____ 7. mummification

a. what the Egyptians called the desert surrounding their country

b. the process of preserving a dead body by drying it

c. rich soil deposited by a river

d. what the Egyptians called their country, referring to its fertile soil

e. a writing system where pictures stand for words

f. the area of the Nile River where silt is deposited before the water empties into the Mediterranean

g. paper-like material made from reeds

Multiple Choice

8. The Egyptian Civilization developed along the banks of which river?

   a. the Danube

   b. the Indus

   c. the Congo

   d. the Nile

9. Which Wonder of the Ancient World is still standing today?

   a. the Sphinx

   b. the Great Pyramid of Giza

   c. the Lighthouse of Alexandria

   d. the Hanging Gardens of Babylon

10. Which Egyptian structure had the face of a human and the body of a lion?

   a. the Sphinx

   b. the Great Pyramid of Giza

   c. the Lighthouse of Alexandria

   d. the tomb of King Tut

Constructed Response

11. Why did the Egyptians mummify their dead? Use details from the reading selection to help support your answer.

_____

_____

_____

_____

_____

_____

_____

Egypt's Three Kingdoms

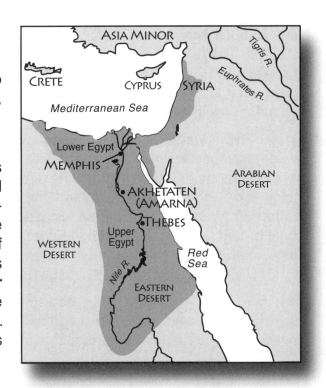

The Egyptian Civilization is generally divided into three periods: the Old Kingdom, the Middle Kingdom, and the New Kingdom.

THE OLD KINGDOM

The first period of the Egyptian Civilization is called the **Old Kingdom**. It lasted from 3100 B.C. until 2040 B.C. Before 3100 B.C., Egypt was really two different kingdoms—Upper Egypt and Lower Egypt. These names are deceiving because if you look at a map of this ancient country, you will see that **Lower Egypt** was located in the north at the top of the map and **Upper Egypt** was located in the south at the bottom of the map. This is because the Nile flows from south to north. It flows parallel to the Red Sea and eventually empties into the Mediterranean Sea.

The First Dynasty

About 3100 B.C., King Menes, a king from the south, was credited with combining the Upper and Lower Kingdoms and uniting Egypt. Menes became the first pharaoh of Egypt. **Pharaoh** was the term given to the king or ruler in Egypt. Menes was the first king of the first dynasty of Egypt. Eventually there would be thirty dynasties to rule Egypt. A **dynasty** is a series of rulers from the same family or line.

During the Old Kingdom, pharaohs were considered gods. They owned the land and everything in the country. They could do anything they wanted and make any law they wanted to. This was called the "divine rights of kings." Many pyramids were built during the Old Kingdom as tombs for the pharaohs. One of the most important pyramids was the Great Pyramid of Giza, built for the pharaoh called Khufu or Cheops.

Menes made Memphis the capital of Egypt. To help run the large country, Menes assigned people he trusted to govern different sections of Egypt. These governors, or **nomarchs**, worked to be sure that all of the commands of the pharaoh were obeyed.

In order to make communication easier between the pharaoh in Memphis and the nomarchs in various parts of the kingdom, the Egyptians developed a written language called hieroglyphics. **Hieroglyphics** uses pictures of objects, such as animals or plants, to represent words. The Egyptian writers, or scribes, wrote their messages and kept records on a paper-like material made from the papyrus reed.

The Nomarchs Gain Power

About 2200 B.C., the nomarchs began to act more independently and obeyed the king less. Many broke away from Egypt, establishing their own provinces. Some of the nomarchs fought each other over territory. Eventually two separate kingdoms were established.

The Book of the Dead

THE MIDDLE KINGDOM

In 2040 B.C., King Mentuhotep of the 11th dynasty reunited Egypt. He created a centralized monarchy, which launched the period known as the **Middle Kingdom**. He made Thebes his capital. The nomarchs lost power, and Egypt again became a centralized government. The pharaoh had all of the power in the country.

Things went well for the Egyptians during this time. Egypt became prosperous. New quarries were developed in order to build more temples and other structures. They built dams and a reservoir to manage the flood water. They expanded their kingdom south to Nubia. Egyptians brought gold, ivory, and slaves from Nubia. They also expanded trade during this period. The Egyptians traded with those living in the Middle East, along the Mediterranean, and in other locations. This trade brought peace and wealth to Egypt. Egyptians had time to create works of art, build temples, develop crafts, and practice their religion.

The Middle Kingdom ended in about 1800 B.C. when Egypt was conquered by the **Hyksos** from Canaan. The Hyksos were good soldiers and had superior weapons. The Hyksos had horse-drawn chariots and curved swords called scimitars, which were made of bronze. The wooden weapons of the Egyptians were no match for these modern weapons.

THE NEW KINGDOM

The third period of the Egyptian Civilization is called the **New Kingdom**, and it lasted from 1600 B.C. until 1100 B.C. This is considered the last great period in Egyptian history. You probably noticed that the Middle Kingdom ended about 1800 B.C. and the New Kingdom began about 1600 B.C. What happened to those 200 years in between? Did Egypt cease to exist? In a way it did. During this time, Egypt was conquered by the Hyksos, who had superior weapons. Eventually, the Egyptians began using these newer weapons as well and were able to win their country back from the Hyksos. Egypt was united once more, and the New Kingdom, sometimes called the Golden Age of Egypt or the Age of Empire, began. Egyptian armies conquered Syria, Palestine, and the area west of the Euphrates River, and Egypt became wealthy.

Artifact from King Tut's Tomb

Pharaoh Amenhotep IV forced the people to worship only one god, the sun god Aten. He closed the temples of other gods and had workmen remove the plural word "gods" from buildings and from other structures. He changed his own name to Akhenate, which means "spirit of Aten." He created a new capital named Akhetaton, devoted to the god. When Akhenate died, Pharaoh Tutankhamen (Tut) restored the old gods and made Thebes the capital again.

Beginning in 1070 B.C., the Egyptian Empire began to decline. There was a civil war. Egypt also had to defend itself from many different invasions over the years. Egyptians fought the Hittites, the Lybians, the Nubians, and the "sea peoples," invaders from somewhere in the Mediterranean. Over a period of time, the Egyptians were invaded by the Assyrians in 671 B.C. and the Persians in 525 B.C. Alexander the Great conquered Egypt in 332 B.C. and installed Ptolemy, a non-Egyptian ruler. Ptolemy's dynasty ruled until the Romans invaded in 32 B.C.

Name: _____   Date: _____

Knowledge Check

Matching

_____ 1. Lower Egypt
_____ 2. Upper Egypt
_____ 3. pharaoh
_____ 4. dynasty
_____ 5. nomarchs
_____ 6. hieroglyphics
_____ 7. Hyksos

a. the king or ruler of Egypt
b. governors of different sections of Egypt
c. kingdom located in the southern part of Egypt
d. invaders from Canaan who had superior bronze weapons and horse-drawn chariots
e. kindgom located in the northern part of Egypt
f. a series of rulers from the same family or line
g. a writing system where pictures stand for words

Multiple Choice

8. During which period did Egypt expand south to Nubia and increase their trading throughout the region?
   a. New Kingdom
   b. Middle Kingdom
   c. Old Kingdom
   d. Upper Kingdom

9. During which period did King Menes unite the kingdoms and become the first king of the first dynasty of Egypt?
   a. New Kingdom
   b. Middle Kingdom
   c. Old Kingdom
   d. Upper Kingdom

10. During which period did Pharaoh Amenhotep IV create a new capital at Akhetaton and force everyone to worship only the sun god Aten?
    a. New Kingdom
    b. Middle Kingdom
    c. Old Kingdom
    d. Upper Kingdom

Constructed Response

11. Egypt was a large kingdom to rule. Describe some of the things that happened as a result of trying to run such a large country. Use details from the reading selection to help support your answer.

_____

_____

_____

_____

_____

_____

The Far East: China

Civilization Develops Along Chinese Rivers

Along with Mesopotamia, ancient Egypt, and the Indus Valley, ancient China was one of the world's earliest civilizations. The Chinese civilization developed on the banks of major rivers. The fertile land beside rivers provided rich soil for farming and hunting and water for drinking, irrigating crops, and fishing. The civilization of ancient China developed along the Huang He (Hwang Ho), or Yellow River. The Huang He is the second-longest river in China. It flows east from the Tibetan highlands to the Yellow Sea in north China, with a length of about 3,000 miles. Villages also developed along the Chang Jiang (Yangtze), the longest river in China.

The **Huang He** is sometimes called the Yellow River because of the color of the yellow mud it carries. Like the Nile, each year the Huang He overflows its banks, and when the flood water recedes, fertile mud is left behind. Crops grow well in this fertile soil, so it is not surprising that by around 5000 B.C., agricultural villages began to spring up along this river.

The Xia (Hsia) Dynasty

The Chinese civilization began about 8000 years ago and still exists today. Since China's history is so long, space does not permit us to consider anything but the beginning of this intriguing civilization. The **Xia (Hsia) Dynasty** is considered to be the first dynasty of kings to rule China. The Xia Dynasty lasted from around 2205 to 1766 B.C. During this period, the Chinese civilization developed in a manner similar to the civilizations in the Near East. The Chinese built irrigation canals to water their crops, they made bronze, harvested silk, used the potter's wheel, and the soldiers used chariots.

The Shang Dynasty

The Xia Dynasty was eventually replaced with the **Shang Dynasty**. The Shang Dynasty lasted from about 1766 to 1122 B.C. During this period, cities were carefully planned, and the people were divided into social ranks that ranged from royalty and nobles to slaves. While most people during this dynasty were farmers, craftsmen became more popular. Bronze-casting was developed at about this time.

Silk and the Trade Routes

During the ten major dynasties that followed the Shang Dynasty, trade flourished. Trade routes between Asia and the West were established, and silk became the main export of China. **Silk** is a very thin cloth made from cocoons spun by silkworms. The trade routes to West Asia and Europe became known as the **Silk Roads**. Other countries wanted to make silk for themselves, but the Chinese kept their methods of producing this cloth a secret until the fourth century A.D.

Preparing Newly Woven Silk

Chinese Religion

In ancient China, there were many gods, such as the earth god, the rain god, and the river god, but there was one god that was revered above all others. This was **Shang Ti**, "the Ruler Above."

The Chinese made sacrifices to the gods to ensure good crops, success in battle, and good fortune. While the poor could only present food and wine to the gods in their temples, the rich sacrificed animals. On special occasions, such as the death of a king, humans were sacrificed. The humans who were sacrificed were often prisoners of war or slaves.

The ancient Chinese believed that when a person died, he or she went to live with Shang Ti. They believed their dead ancestors had powers to help them make wise decisions or to punish them. Therefore, the Chinese worshipped their ancestors. To please their ancestors, the Chinese built temples. They held many celebrations to honor their ancestors.

Chinese Philosophers

Perhaps as great as the technological contributions the Chinese made to the world were the philosophical contributions made by two great teachers who lived in China. One was **Confucius**, who lived from 551 B.C. to 479 B.C. Among other things, Confucius taught politeness, sincerity, unselfishness, respect for laws, and hard work. His beliefs have been written down, and his philosophy has become a religion called **Confucianism**.

Confucius

Another philosopher who lived about the same time as Confucius was **Lao-tzu**. His beliefs were quite different from Confucius. Confucius thought people should improve society, but Lao-tzu taught that people should withdraw from society. He believed that people should live very simple lives in harmony with nature. He thought people should not try to be famous or rich but to be happy with what they had. He also thought people should sit quietly and meditate. His philosophy is called **Taoism** and comes from the word "tao," which means "way."

The Great Wall of China

One of the great achievements of the ancient Chinese Civilization was the construction of the **Great Wall of China**. It was built to keep out invaders. It consists of two stone walls that average about ten feet apart and run parallel to each other. The area between the walls is filled with earth and lined with stone, forming a road. The wall, which ran along the border between China and the territories in the north, is about 30 feet high and 1,500 miles long. Many separate walls were built over 2,000 years. It began as an earthen wall supported by planks. It was built in segments by different states and each was only a few miles long. In about 221 B.C., **Shi Huang Ti**, the first emperor of China, had these walls linked into one long wall. The stone wall as we know it today began during the **Ming Dynasty**, which lasted from A.D. 1368 to 1644. This wall was strong, over 4,500 miles long, and was patrolled by 100,000 soldiers. However, over the years, parts of the wall have been taken down and used to build other structures.

The Great Wall of China

Chinese Inventions

The Chinese invented many things. Some of these include the magnetic compass, crossbow, matches, movable type, paper money, acupuncture, propeller, gunpowder, porcelain, umbrella, paper, wheelbarrow, seismograph, kite, cast iron, abacus, rocket, brandy, whiskey, the game of chess, and many others.

Name: _____ Date: _____

Knowledge Check

Matching

_____ 1. Huang He

_____ 2. silk

_____ 3. Silk Roads

_____ 4. Shang Ti

_____ 5. Confucianism

_____ 6. Taoism

_____ 7. Great Wall of China

_____ 8. Shi Huang Ti

a. river that flows from the Tibetan Highlands to the Yellow Sea; also called the Yellow River

b. religion developed by the philosopher Confucius

c. a very thin cloth made from cocoons spun by worms

d. the first emperor of China

e. trade routes from China to West Asia and Europe

f. the most important Chinese god; "the Ruler Above"

g. built to keep out invaders; built over a period of 2000 years; over 4,500 miles at its longest

h. philosophy developed by Lao-tzu

Multiple Choice

9. During which period was the Great Wall of China strengthened into a stone wall that was over 4,500 miles long?

a. Xia (Hsia) Dynasty

b. Shang Dynasty

c. Ming Dynasty

d. Chin Dynasty

10. Which Chinese philosopher taught that people should withdraw from society and live very simple lives in harmony with nature?

a. Shi Huang Ti

b. Lao-tzu

c. Confucius

d. Shang Ti

11. Which item was NOT something invented by the Chinese?

a. microscope

b. crossbow

c. gunpowder

d. paper

Constructed Response

12. Why did the ancient Chinese worship their ancestors? Use details from the reading selection to help support your answer.

_____

_____

_____

_____

_____

_____

_____

Name: _____ Date: _____

Explore: Reproduce a Chinese Invention

The Chinese invented many things. Here are some Chinese inventions you can make.

MAKE A KITE

Kites were more than toys. They were very important tools in ancient China. Kites were used in construction. Materials were lifted with a kite. Kites were used in battles as well. Messages attached to kites were flown over enemy lines until they reached their allies, and then the lines were cut, and the kites and the messages fell to the soldiers below. Kites with hooks and bait were used for fishing. Kites were even fitted with whistles to make musical sounds while flying.

Listed below are simple directions for making a kite. While a kite made in this way may fly, it will not be very durable. The purpose is to make a very colorful kite that might be similar to one made by the ancient Chinese. Directions for more durable and more sophisticated kites can be found online or in craft books.

Materials:
- Large sheet of construction paper
- String
- Paint
- Tissue or crepe paper

Directions:
- Fold the construction paper in half.
- Draw and cut out half the shape of your kite on one half of the paper. You might choose the shape of a butterfly, bird, or dragon. Unfold the paper to reveal the whole shape.
- Color your kite with watercolors or finger paint.
- When dry, tie the string to one end and attach tissue paper scraps to make a tail.

MAKE A BALLOON ROCKET

The Chinese originally used gunpowder for fireworks, but then they developed rockets that could be used in war. The materials needed are common household items.

Materials:
- Balloon
- String
- Paper clip
- Tape
- Drinking straw

Directions:
- Inflate the balloon and close the end with a paper clip.
- Carefully tape the straw to the side of the balloon.
- Thread the string through the straw, stretch the string straight, and then tie the ends of the string to two different chairs that are placed apart.
- Release the paper clip.
- Since the air inside the balloon pushes out in all directions, when the paper clip is removed, the air escapes out the open end. As the air escapes in one direction, it will push the balloon in the opposite direction along the string.

Name: _____ Date: _____

Explore: Reproduce a Chinese Invention (cont.)

MAKE A COMPASS

The magnetic needle compass made sea navigation possible. While this invention revolutionized history, you can make one in a few minutes with materials you have around your house.

Materials:
- Needle
- Magnet
- Cup of water
- Tape
- Slice of cork
- Marking pen

Directions:
- Magnetize the needle by stroking one end of a magnet along the entire length of it about 20 or 30 times. Always stroke in the same direction.
- Tape the needle to a broad, flat cork, and float the cork in the cup of water. The needle will rotate until it's pointing in a north-south direction. Since you probably know which general direction is north, use the magic marker to place a spot on the end of the needle that points to the north.

MAKE MOVABLE TYPE

The Chinese invented printing with movable type, which made it possible to publish books faster and cheaper. This was four hundred years before Gutenberg printed the Bible. Because of the complexity of Chinese writing, however, it was not widely used.

Materials needed to make a printing block:
- Sharp kitchen knife, which should be used only under the supervision of the teacher
- One small, unpeeled potato
- Marking pen
- Paper
- Water
- Small sponge
- Tempera or acrylic paint
- Newspaper

Directions:
- The student or teacher should cut the potato in half.
- With the marker, draw your initials on the part of the potato you have just cut. Since the stamp will print backwards, make sure you draw your initials backwards.
- Either the student or teacher should cut away the potato around the initials you drew. Make sure the initials stick up about 1/4 inch.
- Dampen the sponge and then dip it in paint.
- Place the sponge on the newspaper, press your stamp against the sponge, and then press the stamp against your paper. Your initials should be printed. It may be necessary to recarve part of your initials if they are not quite right.

The Mongols

Mongol Hunters, Including Kublai Khan, one of Genghis Khan's Grandsons

Living on the Steppes

Just north of the Gobi Desert, between Siberia and northwest China, is a large area called the steppes. The word *steppe* is a Slavic word that means "grasslands." The steppe is a harsh land that is very hot in the summer and very cold in the winter. Temperatures range from 40 degrees below zero in the winter to over 100 degrees in the summer. In the 11th century A.D., the steppe was home to several nomadic tribes. One of these tribes was the **Mongols**. As **nomadic** people, they moved as the seasons changed in order to have grass for grazing their sheep and horses.

For many centuries, the Mongols were a number of independent tribes who often fought with one another. All of the Mongol tribes were made up of excellent horsemen, and some included hunters. With their horses, they chased deer and antelope and were able to either kill them with arrows or lasso them. All of these qualities made the Mongols outstanding warriors.

The Mongols Unite Under Genghis Khan

The Chinese feared the Mongol warriors and built a great wall to keep them out, but the Mongols often scaled the wall and attacked them anyway. Early in the 13th century, China's greatest fear came to pass. The independent Mongolian tribes that they feared were united by Genghis Khan into a powerful nation eager to expand its empire.

At birth he was called **Temujin**, but he gave himself the title "**Genghis Khan**" when he became chief of his tribe. Genghis Khan means "mighty lord." Genghis Khan was an excellent general and one of the greatest conquerors of all time. He was disciplined, well organized, and planned his **strategy** carefully. Genghis Khan's ability, coupled with the use of modern weapons, enabled the Mongol armies to be victorious despite being outnumbered in most of their battles.

Genghis Khan

In 1211, Genghis Khan led the Mongols in an invasion of the Chin Empire in northern China. This first raid led to many others, and eventually the empire covered an area that included the countries that today are known as Mongolia, China, Korea, Russia, India, much of the Middle East, and all the area in between.

The Mongols were known for their brutality. They routinely destroyed everything that stood in their path. Everyone was the enemy. They not only killed soldiers, but also women, children, and animals. They would sometimes conquer a town, kill everyone in it, and then burn it down.

After Genghis Khan died in 1227, the empire was divided among his four sons, and it continued to expand. The grandsons of Genghis Khan successfully conquered most of Asia and parts of Europe. The Mongol Empire became the largest empire the world has ever known. This enormous empire was difficult to maintain and administer, though. Eventually, the conquered people became stronger and were able to drive the Mongols out of their lands.

> **MONGOL CIVILIZATION AT A GLANCE**
> **WHERE:** Steppe region between Siberia and northwest China
> **WHEN:** A.D. 1206–1368
> **ACHIEVEMENTS:**
> - Had the largest contiguous empire in world history (9,300,000 sq. mi)
> - Excellent horsemen
> - Fierce warriors

Name: _____ Date: _____

Knowledge Check

Matching

_____ 1. steppe

_____ 2. Mongols

_____ 3. nomadic

_____ 4. Temujin

_____ 5. Genghis Khan

_____ 6. strategy

a. the name Genghis Khan was given at birth

b. careful plan for how to fight a battle or deal with an enemy

c. name that means "mighty lord"; leader of the Mongols

d. harsh grassland between Siberia and northwest China

e. moving from place to place with no permanent home; often moving with the seasons to find food

f. one of the nomadic tribes of the Asian steppe who united under Genghis Khan to become a nation of fierce warriors and conquer the largest empire in world history

Multiple Choice

7. Who built a great wall to try to keep the Mongols from invading their territory?

   a. the Russians

   b. the Koreans

   c. the Tibetans

   d. the Chinese

8. What did the Mongols use to hunt and chase deer and antelope?

   a. horses

   b. sheep

   c. dogs

   d. cats

9. The Mongol Empire became its largest under whose rule?

   a. Genghis Khan's

   b. Genghis Khan's nephews'

   c. Genghis Khan's grandsons'

   d. Genghis Khan's sons'

Constructed Response

10. Describe how large the Mongol Empire was at its height. Use details from the reading selection to help support your answer.

_____

_____

_____

_____

_____

_____

_____

_____

The Indus Valley

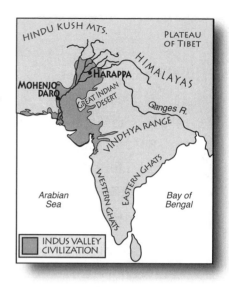

The Harappan or Indus Civilization

The fertility of the **Indus Valley** lured farmers to the river's banks in about 2500 B.C. The people who lived along the Indus River developed one of the world's first great urban civilizations. Archaeologists call this civilization the **Harappan Culture** or **Indus Valley Civilization**. This civilization originated in what is today Pakistan and western India and developed at about the same time as the early city-states of Egypt and Mesopotamia. Unlike those other civilizations, very little was known about the Indus Valley Civilization until recently. In 1921, an Indian archaeologist discovered remnants of a large city named Harappa.

Harappa and Mohenjo-daro

Harappa was one of the centers of the Indus Valley Civilization. The other, located about 350 miles away, was **Mohenjo-daro**. These two large cities were the homes of merchants and

Mohenjo-daro today

craftsmen. Ruins from these cities indicate the people of this culture planned their cities carefully before they built them. The buildings and streets were neatly arranged according to a grid system. Each city had a large **granary** and water tank as well as homes made of bricks and plaster. The houses were large with several rooms that led into a courtyard. Some of the homes had wells for drinking water and bathing, bathrooms with toilets, and a system for drainage. In fact, the builders of Mohenjo-daro designed and built one of the world's first drainage and sewage systems for a city.

Farming

The people of the Indus Valley Civilization built a complex system of canals and dams for irrigation and flood management. They practiced **communal** farming. On these large farms, they grew barley, rice, wheat, dates, and cotton. They were one of the first civilizations known to have domesticated animals. They raised cattle, chickens, and buffalo. The farmers used wheeled carts drawn by oxen to take their grain to the cities where it was stored in large granaries.

Trading

Those who did not farm or hunt were either tradesmen or craftsmen. They bought gold from southern India, turquoise from Iran, silver and copper from Afghanistan, and jade from India. With these goods, craftsmen were able to make pottery, jewelry, sculptures, spears, and knives.

The Civilization Declines

About 1750 B.C. the civilization began to decline. Earthquakes and floods destroyed the irrigation system, and many buildings were also destroyed. For some reason, the people did not rebuild. Invaders caused many to abandon the Indus Valley. Although nomads lived in this region for a while, hundreds of years would pass before new cities were built.

> ### INDUS VALLEY CIVILIZATION AT A GLANCE
>
> **WHERE:** Western part of South Asia in what is now Pakistan and western India
>
> **WHEN:** 2500 B.C.–1750 B.C.
>
> **ACHIEVEMENTS:**
> - Built dams and canals for irrigation
> - Well-planned cities
> - One of the world's first drainage and sewer systems for a city
> - Among the first people to cultivate cotton
> - Among the first people to domesticate animals

Name: _____ Date: _____

Knowledge Check

Matching

_____ 1. Indus Valley

_____ 2. Harappan Culture

_____ 3. Harappa

_____ 4. Mohenjo-daro

_____ 5. granary

_____ 6. communal

a. a place to store grain

b. one of the centers of the Indus Valley Civilization; rediscovered in 1921

c. region in what is now Pakistan and western India, along the Indus River

d. another name for the Indus Valley Civilization

e. shared or used in common by a group or members of a community

f. one of the centers of the Indus Valley Civilization; home to merchants and craftsmen

Multiple Choice

7. Mohenjo-daro is known for having one of the first
   a. city wells.
   b. city walls.
   c. city sewage systems.
   d. city banks.

8. How was grain moved from the fields into the cities?
   a. on men's backs
   b. in wheeled carts pulled by oxen
   c. on llamas
   d. on sleds pulled by men

9. What destroyed the Indus Valleys' irrigation system?
   a. earthquakes and floods
   b. a volcano
   c. hurricanes
   d. invaders

10. Where would Indus Valley traders get turquoise?
    a. India
    b. Afghanistan
    c. China
    d. Iran

Constructed Response

11. What evidence is there that the Indus Valley cities were well planned? Use details from the reading selection to help support your answer.

_____

_____

_____

_____

_____

The Aegean Civilizations

Greece and the Aegean Sea

The civilizations that developed around Greece and the islands in the Aegean Sea are often called the **Aegean Civilizations**. While there is evidence that humans lived in Greece over 8,000 years ago, it wasn't until about 3000 B.C. that the earliest signs of civilization actually began. Greek civilization can be divided into three distinct periods.

1. The **Early Period** is sometimes called the Bronze Age. This period lasted from 3000 B.C. to 1150 B.C. Many of the legends written by Homer were stories that supposedly happened in this period.
   - The **Minoan** culture thrived on the island of Crete from sometime before 2000 B.C. to 1450 B.C.
   - The **Mycenaean** culture developed on the Greek mainland and reached its height about 1600 B.C. It lasted for about 400 years.

2. The **Middle Period** is sometimes called the Dark Ages. It lasted from about 1100 B.C. until about 800 B.C. During the Middle Period, the culture declined. The people living in what we call Greece organized themselves not into one great nation, but rather into several city-states. Each city-state was a separate unit that governed itself.

3. The **Classical Period** began about 800 B.C. and lasted until 323 B.C. This is the period that includes the Golden Age of Greece when democracy, drama, philosophy, science, literature, and other accomplishments of this great culture reached their peaks. The city-states of Athens and Sparta, which represented two very different ideals, thrived during the Classical Period. The period ended with the death of Alexander the Great, who had conquered Persia and spread the Greek culture from Egypt to India. Eventually, the Romans conquered all of the land that had belonged to Greece.

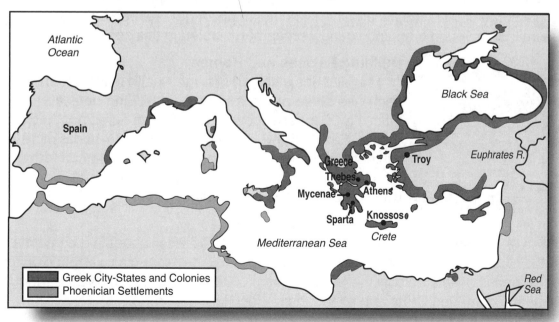

The Early Period: The Minoans

Named after their king Minos, the **Minoan Civilization** was the first civilization in Europe. It was located on the island of Crete and other islands in the Aegean Sea from sometime before 2000 B.C. to 1450 B.C. Since Crete is an island and is relatively isolated from the rest of the world, the Minoan Civilization was not too concerned with invasion. They did not have to spend their time and resources developing armies and weapons. They were free to concentrate on economic growth. This made it possible for the Minoans to grow enough food so that not everyone had to farm or hunt. Some were free to create art, fashion jewelry, or to make items that people used. Still others became merchants trading food and items with those living on other Aegean islands and those living on the continent. Minoans **exported** oil, wine, jewelry, and crafts. They **imported** many raw materials.

> **MINOAN CIVILIZATION AT A GLANCE**
> **WHERE:** Crete, a large island between Asia Minor and Greece
> **WHEN:** 2000 B.C.–1450 B.C.
> **ACHIEVEMENTS:**
> - The first civilization in Europe
> - One of the first social cultures with social equality
> - Built elaborate palaces and large homes for its citizens
> - Women were treated more fairly than in other cultures of the time

Social Equality

The wealth produced by trade had two effects, which were very unusual in the ancient world. The first was **social equality**. In most ancient civilizations, there were distinct classes, such as the nobility, the priests, and the poor. On Crete, while some were wealthier than others, most people prospered enough to have enough food and live in fairly large homes. Even women seemed to be treated well, which was rare in the ancient world.

Leisure Time

The second benefit of wealth was that the Minoans had **leisure time** to devote to activities not directly related to survival. Free from the worries of finding food and shelter, many Minoans became interested in other activities and sports, such as boxing and bull-jumping. **Bull-jumping** involved a jumper taking a charging bull by the horns and either jumping onto the bull's back or leaping over the bull, turning a somersault in the air, and then landing on his or her feet behind or beside the bull. Both young men and young women participated in this sport.

Minoan children boxing

Building Palaces and Homes

The Minoans also had enough wealth to build many towns, with each one centered on a large palace. One palace at the island's main city, **Knossos**, covered over three acres and had over 1,000 rooms. Some of the Minoan palaces even had simple plumbing systems with toilets. Minoans also built large comfortable homes for all the people, including the poor. Most homes were two stories with some up to five stories high.

Part of the Palace of Knossos Reconstructed

The Defeat of the Minoans

The Minoans thrived on Crete for about five centuries. Then in 1450 B.C., they were conquered by the Mycenaeans, who had developed a civilization on the Greek mainland. No one is quite sure why the Minoans were conquered. Some think an earthquake, volcano, or tsunami damaged Crete and ruined their agriculture and trade.

Name: _____ Date: _____

Knowledge Check

Matching

_____	1. Minoan Civilization	a.	brought into a country
_____	2. exported	b.	activities not directly related to survival
_____	3. imported	c.	sent out of a country
_____	4. social equality	d.	the main city of Crete that had a huge palace
_____	5. leisure time	e.	the first civilization in Europe; on the island of Crete and other islands in the Aegean Sea
_____	6. bull-jumping	f.	grabbing a bull by the horns, flipping over it, and landing on one's feet on the ground
_____	7. Knossos	g.	when all people in a society are treated the same

Multiple Choice

8. Since the Minoans lived on islands, they did not have to worry as much about developing what?

    a. trade   b. armies

    c. agriculture   d. art

9. Who was the king of the Minoan Civilization for whom it was named?

    a. Menelaus   b. Agamemnon

    c. Theseus   d. Minos

10. What was unusual about Crete's social structure?

    a. Women were treated well.   b. It was divided into distinct classes.

    c. The poor were cast out of town.   d. The nobles had most of the wealth.

Constructed Response

11. What were some of the benefits of the Minoans not having to concentrate all their efforts on producing food, finding shelter, and defending against invaders? Use details from the reading selection to help support your answer.

_____

_____

_____

_____

_____

_____

_____

The Early Period: The Mycenaeans

The **Mycenaeans** arrived in Greece about 2000 B.C. and lived on the mainland. Their civilization actually began around 1650 B.C., but they did not become dominant in the area until about 1450 B.C. Their supremacy lasted only approximately 200 years. In about 1200 B.C., they were attacked and their palaces were destroyed. We do not know who conquered the Mycenaeans.

The city of Mycenae was protected by huge stone walls.

Mycenaean Cities Prepared for War

The best-known city of this civilization was **Mycenae**. The Mycenaeans traded heavily with the Minoans on Crete and were strongly influenced by their culture. In 1450 B.C. when the Mycenaeans conquered the Minoans, they adopted much of the Minoan culture. One major difference between the Minoans and the Mycenaeans was their architecture. While the Minoan cities and palaces were unfortified, Mycenaean cities were heavily **fortified** and protected by huge stone walls. Invaders were common in Greece, and there were many wars.

Trade

Mycenaeans became rich by trading. The excess food they produced was traded on various islands and in cities on the mainland around the Mediterranean. In return, the Mycenaeans imported copper, tin, gold, and other items. They were so ambitious that they traded as far away as Mesopotamia and Western Europe. There is even evidence their trade may have extended as far away as Scandinavia and Russia. In addition to traders, they were warriors and mercenaries.

Homer's Epic Poems

The *Iliad* and the *Odyssey* are long poems called **epic poems** written by **Homer**, the blind Greek poet who lived in about 800 B.C. These poems are about Mycenaean heroes. The Greeks believed these stories had actually happened. While there may have been some truth in the stories, it is likely that each generation added to the stories to make them more interesting and heroic. Homer was the first to write down the stories because there had been no alphabet before the Greeks learned the Phoenician alphabet.

Mask of Agamemnon

The *Iliad*

The *Iliad* tells of King Agamemnon of Mycenae and how he and a group of Greek heroes went to war with Troy, a city on the coast of what is now Turkey. Legend says the war was fought over the kidnapping of Helen, the beautiful queen and wife of Menelaus. He was Agamemnon's brother and the King of Sparta. Historians believe the war was probably fought over land. The Trojan War lasted for ten years. Finally, the Greeks tricked the Trojans into bringing a wooden horse into the city. Greek soldiers hidden in the horse opened the gates to the city, and the Greek army entered the city and defeated the Trojans.

The *Odyssey*

The **Odyssey** is the story of Odysseus and his long journey home after the Trojan War. During his journey, which lasted ten years, he had many adventures that involved gods, goddesses, and mortals.

MYCENAEAN CIVILIZATION AT A GLANCE

WHERE: On the mainland of Greece

WHEN: 1650 B.C.–1200 B.C.

ACHIEVEMENTS:

- Their leaders, warriors, and wars serve as the basis for much of Homer's *Illiad* and *Odyssey*
- The first Greek-speaking people
- Excellent traders and craftsmen

Name: _____ Date: _____

Knowledge Check

Matching

_____ 1. Mycenaeans
_____ 2. Mycenae
_____ 3. fortified
_____ 4. epic poem
_____ 5. Homer
_____ 6. *Iliad*
_____ 7. *Odyssey*

a. people who arrived on the mainland of Greece about 2000 B.C. and became dominant about 1450 B.C.

b. blind Greek poet who wrote epic poems about Mycenaean heroes

c. the story of a Mycenaean soldier's journey home after the Trojan War

d. protected by huge stone walls

e. the best-known city of the Mycenaean Civilization

f. the story of the war between Greece and Troy

g. long poem that tells a story

Multiple Choice

8. What made the Mycenaeans rich?
   a. trading
   b. writing
   c. going to war
   d. mining

9. Where did the Greeks get the alphabet they began to use for their writing?
   a. the Minoans
   b. the Phoenicians
   c. the Egyptians
   d. the Persians

10. In the *Iliad*, what was the legendary cause of the Trojan War?
   a. a fight over land
   b. an argument over trade
   c. the trick of the wooden horse
   d. the kidnapping of Helen

Critical Thinking

11. Why do you think the stories that Homer wrote were so different from what actually happened? Use details from the reading selection to help support your answer.

_____
_____
_____
_____
_____
_____

Name: _____ Date: _____

Explore: Greek Word Roots

Many of the words we use every day were taken from the Greeks. Below is a sample of some of the words that had their origins in ancient Greece. To the left is the definition of the word. You are to fill in the blanks at the right to complete the word that goes with the definition. Use a dictionary or an online resource if you need help.

DEFINITION	TERM
1. Another name for a play	__ R __ M __
2. A long and adventurous trip	O D Y __ __ E Y
3. An institution designed for learning	__ __ __ O O __
4. Plain and simple	S P __ __ __ __ N
5. A room for indoor sports	__ Y __ __ __ S I U __
6. Keeps a boat in place	__ __ C H __ __
7. A funny play	C __ __ __ __ __
8. A play in which the main character suffers	T __ __ G __ __ __
9. A person who writes poetry	__ __ __ T
10. The study of numbers	__ __ T H __ __ __ T __ __ __
11. A system of values	P H __ __ __ S __ __ __ __
12. Another name for a dictator	__ Y R __ __ T
13. A person who rules	__ O N A __ __ H
14. The study of living things	__ __ __ __ __ G Y
15. A group of musicians playing together	__ R __ __ __ __ T R __
16. A name for an actor or actress	T __ __ S P __ __ N
17. The study of the effect of civilization on the environment	E __ __ __ __ __ Y
18. A brave person	__ __ __ O
19. The science of managing government	__ __ L __ __ I C S
20. Mathematics dealing with lines, angles, and solids	G __ O __ __ T R __
21. A course dealing with the rules of language	__ __ __ M M __ R
22. Government where all citizens help make decisions	D __ __ __ __ C R __ __ __
23. A cruel or mean leader	D __ C T __ __ __ R
24. This prevents the growth of germs	A N T __ __ __ P __ __ C
25. A building where people worship	__ __ U R __ __
26. One of a number of related events	E P __ S O __ __

The Middle Period: Athens and Sparta

This Athenian sculpture dates to 600 B.C.

The Dark Ages

After the fall of Mycenaea, Greece entered the **Middle Period**, which is sometimes called the **Dark Ages**. It lasted from about 1100 B.C. until about 800 B.C. During the Middle Period, the culture declined. Little is known about this period in Greek history since there are no written records.

The Polis

We do know there were various groups of people living in villages on the mainland as well as the islands in the Aegean Sea. Since these villages were separated by mountains and the sea, there was little contact among the various villages. As a result, each village was concerned with its own needs, not caring at all about those living in other villages. Gradually, the people organized them-selves into several small city-states, almost like separate nations, each called a **polis**. Each polis was a separate unit that developed its own government. It not only consisted of the city, but included the area surrounding the city as well. Each polis had a marketplace called an **agora**. An area that was higher than the rest of the polis was called an **acropolis**. A wall to protect the polis was often built.

Greek Civilization

We consider all of the city-states in Greece to be the Greek Civilization, because they shared the same language, religion, and culture. However, the Greeks living in this time were not loyal to Greece as a nation, but to the city-state in which they lived. Many city-states began to develop during the Middle Period, but the best-known and most powerful were Athens and Sparta. People from Athens were called **Athenians**. Those living in Sparta were **Spartans**. Sparta was located on the **Peloponnesian Peninsula** of Greece. Athens was located on the **Attic Peninsula** in a region called Attica.

This figure made in Sparta in approximately 1400 B.C. shows a woman in a typical costume from Crete.

Govenment in Greece

Athens and Sparta were just developing during the Middle Period, and they could not have been more different. One difference between the two was the manner in which they governed themselves. In order to understand how different Athens and Sparta were, it is important to understand how government developed in the Greek city-states. Several different types of government were tried over the years by the Greeks. At one time they had leaders similar to a king, but the people thought they could govern better than one person. So they established an aristocracy. An **aristocracy** is a government by a ruling class. The ruling class in this case was the landowners. This type of government was eventually replaced by an oligarchy. An **oligarchy** is run by only a few people. In the case of the Greeks, the rulers were the wealthiest in town. Many city-states eventually abandoned this type of government and established a democracy. A **democracy** is a government run by the people who are being governed. *Demos* is a Greek word that means "people." In the Greek democracy, all citizens were able to vote and to decide how the city-state was to be run. However, slaves and women were not allowed to vote or participate.

Athens

Athens had a democracy. Every Athenian man, rich or poor, was a member of an assembly, which met to discuss issues concerning Athens. Each citizen was allowed to speak and give his opinion at these assemblies. Each year a council consisting of 500 citizens was chosen by lot. The council managed the city and decided what should be discussed at the assemblies. Citizens also took turns as judges and public officials. This open-minded attitude extended into other aspects of Athenian life. Artists, writers, philosophers, architects, and scientists flourished in Athens.

The Areopagus, on the Acropolis in Athens, was where Athenian democracy was born.

Sparta

Sparta, on the other hand, was ruled by two kings and a council. They did not have a democracy. This type of government worked well for Spartans who were not interested in the "finer things in life" that the Athenians pursued. Spartan life was simple. There was no art, music, poetry, or fine clothing. They cared little for ideas or new invention. Their whole existence was built around war and military discipline. Beginning at age seven, all men were trained as soldiers. They were given little food and were treated harshly to make them ready for the hardships of war. Even women were required to become strong and healthy so that they could have strong and healthy children. The Spartan army was strong and feared throughout the area.

Ruins of Ancient Sparta

Name: _____ Date: _____

Knowledge Check

Matching

_____ 1. Middle Period

_____ 2. polis

_____ 3. agora

_____ 4. acropolis

_____ 5. aristocracy

_____ 6. oligarchy

_____ 7. democracy

a. rule by only a few people

b. rule by a ruling class of people

c. rule by all the people being governed

d. the marketplace of a Greek city

e. an independent Greek city-state

f. time in Greece from about 1100 to 800 B.C.; also called the Dark Ages; culture declined during this time

g. a high place or hill in a Greek city

Multiple Choice

8. Which city-state in Greece encouraged artists, writers, philosophers, architects, and scientists?

   a. Thebes

   c. Athens

   b. Sparta

   d. Mycenae

9. Where were Sparta and Athens located in Greece?

   a. in northern Greece

   c. on Aegean islands

   b. on peninsulas in southern Greece

   d. on the coast of Asia Minor

10. Which city-state in Greece trained its men to be soldiers by giving them little food and treating them harshly?

    a. Thebes

    c. Athens

    b. Sparta

    d. Mycenae

Constructed Response

11. Describe the types of government tried in ancient Greece. Use details from the reading selection to help support your answer.

_____

_____

_____

_____

_____

_____

_____

The Classical Period: The Golden Age of Greece

The **Classical Period** of Greece began about 800 B.C. and lasted until 323 B.C. Although there were periodic wars among the city-states, life was pretty good. Food was in abundance, craftsmen and artists produced objects that could be traded, and the Greeks had enough wealth to devote time to the arts, education, architecture, philosophy, and science. This is the period in which Greek culture reached its peak. It is sometimes called the Golden Age of Greece.

Government

Greeks in Athens valued the world's first democracy they had created. All citizens were members of the governing body called the **assembly**. A citizen was a free man over 21 who was born to Athenian parents. The assembly met every nine days to make decisions on laws, building, and other matters of interest. Each citizen was not only able to vote on the matters that came before the assembly, he also had a right to speak at the assembly in order to influence others.

CLASSICAL GREEK CIVILIZATION AT A GLANCE

WHERE: On the mainland of Greece and surrounding islands. Their influence was expanded to colonies around the Mediterranean Sea.

WHEN: 800 B.C.–323 B.C.

ACHIEVEMENTS:

- Formed the world's first democracy
- Produced the first dramas and developed drama as art
- Built magnificent buildings
- Created beautiful statues
- Wrote literature, poetry, and drama that are so outstanding they are still studied today
- Took a scientific approach to the study of medicine
- Were the first to write histories
- Developed a method of classifying plants
- Developed rules for geometry and made other mathematical contributions

---

This stele shows the personification of Demos crowned by Democracy.

Education

The Greeks understood that it was education that sustained their culture and their good life. However, only young men from wealthy families received an education. When a boy was seven, he was sent to a school. His education was divided into three sections: letters, music, and athletics. The first section of a boy's education, called the **letters**, is what we would call the basics today. Students learned to read, write, and do arithmetic. They also memorized poetry and learned the skill of debating. Music education consisted of learning about music and learning to sing and play a musical instrument. Greeks played the flute and stringed instruments. Girls were also trained to play these instruments. At age 14, boys began their athletic training. They practiced wrestling, jumping, running, and throwing a discus and javelin. This training prepared boys to fight in the army. At age 18, boys were trained as soldiers for two years.

The Parthenon

Children of poor parents and those of slaves were not educated. They began working early in their lives. Girls did not go to school either. Some parents taught them at home. Wealthy parents might hire tutors to teach their daughters to read and write. For the most part, a girl's education consisted of learning to run a home and developing domestic skills.

Religion

The Greeks valued religion. They had many gods who ruled every aspect of their lives. There was a god of war, a god of music, and so on. The king of the gods was Zeus. It was thought that Zeus and all other gods lived on Mount Olympus in the northern part of Greece. The Greeks built magnificent temples in which to worship their gods and made beautiful statues to honor them. They thought their gods were similar to humans, having the same emotions and human qualities. The stories of their gods are called **myths** and are still studied in school.

Drama

Drama, another important part of Greek life, grew out of religion. Greek playwrights developed the art of drama and wrote both **comedies** and **tragedies** in the honor of the gods. These dramas were performed at religious festivals. Some famous Greek playwrights were Euripides, Sophocles, Aeschylus, and Aristophanes.

The Theater of Dionysus

Athletic Games

Athletic contests were held at religious festivals and even at funerals of famous people. The Greeks believed a person should have a healthy mind in a healthy body. Champion athletes were treated as national heroes. The **Olympic Games** originated in Olympia, Greece, in 776 B.C.

Science and Medicine

The Greeks also valued science and medicine. While the Greeks believed that sickness was a punishment of the gods, they did study sick people and diseases and develop treatments based on their research. A famous Greek physician was Hippocrates, who is known as the "Father of Modern Medicine." He is remembered today for the **Hippocratic Oath**, which was named after him. It is an oath that deals with ethics in medicine. Modern doctors still take the Hippocratic Oath before they begin their practices.

Beauty and Knowledge

Magnificent temples, sculpture, painting, music, pottery, and dance flourished during the Classical Period of Greece. Knowledge was as important as beauty. Mathematicians and scientists such as Pythagoras, Heraclitus, and Euclid greatly expanded knowledge of the physical world. There were many great philosophers during this period. Some of the more famous were Socrates, Aristotle, and Plato.

Conflict Between Athens and Sparta

The city-states of Athens and Sparta, which represented two very different ideals, reached their peaks during this period. Both were strong militarily. While Athens had the best navy, Sparta had the best army. In an effort to protect itself from the Persians, the Athenians suggested the various city-states unite into a league. It was named the **Delian League**. The members of the league provided money for an even stronger navy that defeated the Persians in 486 B.C. Athens then sent their navy to attack smaller city-states in order to expand their empire. Sparta and many smaller city-states formed the **Peloponnesian League**. In 431 B.C., the Peloponnesian League declared war on the Delian League.

The **Peloponnesian War** lasted for 27 years. It was costly to all involved. Eventually, Sparta received help from the Persians, and they defeated the Athenians. Sparta began ruling over all of the city-states. Democracy had ended. The Spartans were not good at ruling, however, and for 30 years there were many battles and wars. Greece became so weak that a force from Thebes was able to defeat the Spartans.

Name: _____ Date: _____

Knowledge Check

Matching

_____ 1. Classical Period
_____ 2. assembly
_____ 3. letters
_____ 4. myths
_____ 5. drama
_____ 6. Hippocratic Oath
_____ 7. Olympic Games

a. telling stories through acting and dialog
b. athletic contests started in Greece in 776 B.C.
c. stories about the Greek gods
d. time from 800 to 323 B.C. in Greece; also called the Golden Age of Greece
e. the basics of education; reading, writing, and arithmetic
f. deals with ethics in medicine; doctors still promise to follow its principles
g. a governing body in Athens consisting of all citizens

Multiple Choice

8. What musical instruments did the Greeks play? Circle all that apply.
   a. accordion
   b. stringed instruments
   c. piano
   d. flute

9. Who was known at the "Father of Modern Medicine"?
   a. Hippocrates
   b. Sophocles
   c. Pythagoras
   d. Plato

10. What group did Sparta form that went to war with Athens and her allies?
    a. Delian League
    b. Peloponnesian League
    c. Corinthian League
    d. Persian League

11. Who was able to attend Greek schools?
    a. poor boys
    b. girls
    c. slaves
    d. wealthy boys

Constructed Response

12. How did government in Athens work? Use details from the reading selection to help support your answer.

_____

_____

_____

_____

_____

_____

Name: _____ Date: _____

Explore: Become a Myth Maker

Prior to the ancient Greeks, there was little scientific understanding of the world and how it worked. Stories involving the Greek gods were created to explain things such as thunder, lightning, earthquakes, and other phenomenon. These kinds of stories are called **myths**. Myths involve heroes, gods, and supernatural beings and are used to explain customs, ways of life, or aspects of the world in which we live. A collection of myths is referred to as **mythology**. The Greeks had an extensive mythology that developed from their religion.

In ancient Greece, the people believed that the gods and goddesses lived in a beautiful palace so high on Mount Olympus it could not be seen by humans. The Greeks also believed their gods were immortal, which means they lived forever. According to Greek mythology, there was a god who ruled every aspect of life. Ares was the god of war, Apollo was the god of music, Athena was the goddess of learning, and so on. In addition, there were stories about each of the gods that told how they were born, who their parents were, and what activities they participated in.

ASSIGNMENT: CREATE AN ORIGINAL MYTH

In order to complete this assignment, you will need to read and study a number of Greek myths. You will find that some myths explain a natural phenomenon. Here is an example of a Greek myth that was developed to explain the phenomenon of echoes.

WHY THERE IS AN ECHO

Zeus, the king of the gods, was married to Hera. Hera was very suspicious of Zeus since he had been unfaithful in the past. On one occasion, Hera believed that Zeus was spending time with the wood nymphs and worried that Zeus might be falling in love with them. One day Hera decided to check up on Zeus, but Echo, who was also a nymph, prevented her from searching by engaging her in a long conversation. When Hera realized that Echo's purpose was to prevent her from finding Zeus and the wood nymphs together, she decreed that from that day forward, Echo's speech would be limited to repeating what others said. Echo eventually fell in love with Narcissus, who rejected her. Her grief caused her to gradually fade away until only the sound of her voice remained.

Other myths deal with an emotion such as love, hate, envy, jealousy, or fear. Here is an example of a myth dealing with love and sadness.

ORPHEUS AND EURYDICE

Orpheus (pronounced or-fee-us) was the greatest musician on Earth. Only the gods could play and sing better. Orpheus and a young maiden named Eurydice (pronounced yoo-rid-i-see) fell in love and were married. However, just after the wedding, she was bitten by a viper, and she died. Orpheus was grief-stricken, and he decided to go down to the underworld and plead for his wife to be brought back to life. As he played and sang his request, Hades and the other inhabitants of the underworld were so touched that Hades decided to allow Eurydice to return to the world of the living, but only on one condition. Orpheus could not look at Eurydice until they were both out of the underworld. Orpheus went first, and he didn't look back until he was above ground in the sunshine. However, Eurydice had not yet stepped out of the shadows of the underworld, and as he reached for her, she disappeared back to the underworld. Orpheus was not permitted to enter the underworld again, so he wandered the countryside playing sadly until he too died.

Name: _____ Date: _____

CREATE AN ORIGINAL MYTH

After you have read a few other Greek myths and learned more about the Greek gods and goddesses, you are to write an original Greek myth using one of the Greek gods. Your myth can explain a natural phenomenon, teach a moral truth, or deal with an emotion. Here is a partial list of Greek gods.

CHIEF GREEK GODS AND GODDESSES

1. Zeus - king and father of the gods
2. Poseidon - god of the sea and earthquakes
3. Hera - queen of the gods and guardian of marriage
4. Athena - goddess of wisdom, war, patriotism, good citizenship, and protector of Athens
5. Apollo - god of poetry, music, medicine, and light
6. Artemis - goddess of hunting, wild things, and the moon
7. Ares - god of war
8. Hephaestus - god of fire, the blacksmith god
9. Aphrodite - goddess of love and beauty
10. Hermes - messenger of the gods; god of science and invention
11. Hestia - goddess of the hearth and home
12. Demeter - goddess of grain and agriculture

OTHER IMPORTANT GODS

13. Hades - god of the underworld
14. Eros - god of love (Cupid)
15. Pan - god of the woods and fields (half man and half goat)
16. Dionysus - god of wine, revelry, dancing, and drama

MINOR DIVINITIES

Thalia, the Muse of Comedy

17. Nymphs (Dryads and Nereids) - guarded different parts of nature
18. Muses - goddesses of various arts, mostly literary
    Terpsichore - Muse of choral song and dance
    Euterpe - Muse of lyric poetry
    Erato - Muse of love poetry
    Polyhymnia - Muse of sacred poetry (hymns)
    Thalia - Muse of comic drama
    Calliope - Muse of epic poetry
    Melpomene - Muse of tragic drama
    Urania - Muse of astronomy
    Clio - Muse of history
19. Fates - goddesses who controlled the destiny of every mortal person
    Clotho - spun the bright threads of youth
    Lachesis - distributed the threads of life; directed the destinies of mortals
    Atropos - symbol of death, cut the threads of life

On a separate sheet of paper, answer the following questions and then write your myth.
1. What is the title of your myth?
2. Who are the gods or goddesses involved in your myth?
3. What is your myth about? (emotion, natural phenomenon, moral truth, etc.)

The Macedonians: Alexander the Great

Thebes

For a time, the city-state of Sparta ruled Greece. In a surprising move, the smaller army from **Thebes** was able to defeat them in 371 B.C. The Theban army used a military maneuver, arranging their formation into the shape of a crescent. When the Spartans attacked, the Theban army surrounded them.

Macedonia

Thebes only ruled for a few years, however. In 359 B.C., **Philip II** became king of Macedonia. **Macedonia**, or Macedon as it is sometimes called, was a large area north of Greece. It was a rugged, mountainous country, and the people living there were much different than the Greeks. The Greeks considered themselves very cultured and civilized, but they felt the Macedonians were barbarians.

> **ALEXANDER'S EMPIRE AT A GLANCE**
> **WHERE:** From Greece to India
> **WHEN:** 336 B.C.–323 B.C.
> **ACHIEVEMENTS:**
> - Established the largest empire of the time, which included almost all of the known world
> - Established large cities, including Alexandria, Egypt
> - Spread Greek culture to a large part of the world

Philip strengthened his army and eventually defeated all of the Greek city-states to form one large country. He became the leader of Greece. His goal was to combine the strength of all of the Greeks and defeat the Persians. But in 336 B.C., Philip was assassinated and his son, **Alexander**, became king.

Alexander

Alexander was not only a great warrior, he was also a scholar. His tutor was Aristotle, who trained him in rhetoric, philosophy, history, and literature and encouraged his interest in medicine and science.

Alexander's image engraved on coins

In 336, when Alexander rose to power, the empire was in disorder. Alexander, as well as Macedonia, had many enemies. His first act was to order the execution of those who had killed his father. Then he began to restore order to his small empire. He suppressed a revolt in Thessaly, and he was chosen to be general of the Greek forces. Alexander was only 20 years old at the time.

After uniting the old city-states of Greece, Alexander decided to attack Persia, Greece's old enemy, just as his father had planned. Alexander and his army were successful. The Persian leader, King Darius III, and his army were defeated. Alexander went on to expand his empire by invading Egypt, the Indus Valley, and eastern Iran.

Greek Colonies

Alexander was aware that since his empire was so large, it would be impossible for it to be ruled from a central location, so he established **Greek colonies** in countries he had just defeated. These colonies were run by Alexander's soldiers.

Alexander was returning from his conquests in India when he died of a fever in 323 B.C. He was only 32 years old. In only ten years, he had taken control of almost the entire known world. However, with Alexander dead, the empire began to crumble. His generals killed Alexander's son, and then they fought over the kingdom. Eventually it was divided into three kingdoms—Persia, Macedonia, and Egypt—each ruled by one general. The Greek language and culture remained a dominant part of these areas for several hundred years after the death of Alexander the Great.

Name: _____ Date: _____

Knowledge Check

Matching

_____ 1. Thebes

_____ 2. Philip II

_____ 3. Macedonia

_____ 4. Alexander

_____ 5. Greek colonies

a. a rugged, mountainous area north of Greece

b. the king of Macedonia and Alexander's father

c. outposts set up by Alexander and run by his soldiers in the countries he had defeated

d. rose to power at age 20 and conquered the Persians, Egyptians, and parts of Iran and the Indus Valley

e. defeated Sparta in 371 B.C. and ruled Greece for a few years

Multiple Choice

6. The Greeks considered the Macedonians to be what?

    a. cultured

    c. disciplined soldiers

    b. their allies

    d. barbarians

7. What was Alexander's first act when he rose to power in Macedonia?

    a. He executed his father's killers.

    c. He invaded Persia.

    b. He supressed a revolt in Thassaly.

    d. He defeated the Egyptians.

8. Who was Alexander's tutor who trained him in rhetoric, philosophy, history, literature, medicine, and science?

    a. Philip II

    c. Plato

    b. Aristotle

    d. Socrates

9. Which was NOT one of the kingdoms into which Alexander's empire was divided?

    a. Macedonia

    c. India

    b. Egypt

    d. Persia

Constructed Response

10. Why was Alexander credited with spreading Greek culture to a large part of the world? Use details from the reading selection to help support your answer.

_____

_____

_____

_____

_____

_____

_____

Name: _____ Date: _____

Map Follow-Up: Alexander the Great's Empire

List the modern-day countries that are found in what once was Alexander's empire.

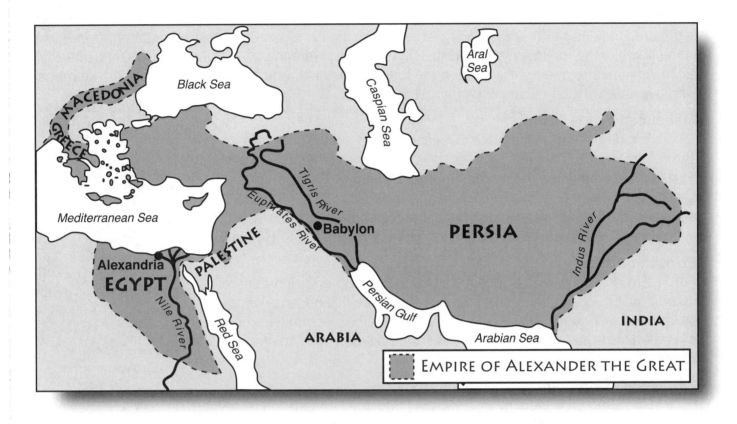

_____

_____

_____

_____

_____

_____

_____

_____

_____

_____

Ancient Europe: The Etruscans

Etruria

The **Etruscans** were an ancient people who lived in what is now central Italy in a region called **Etruria**. They lived between the Tiber River in the south and the Arno River in the north. This is the area Italians call **Tuscany** today. At its height, the Etruscan Culture stretched from Campania in the south to the Po Valley in the north. The Etruscans were in power from about 800 B.C. until 300 B.C. It was the first great civilization on the Italian peninsula, and it greatly influenced the Romans, who overthrew the Etruscan king in about 500 B.C.

Influenced by the Greeks

We do not know where the Etruscans came from. Some believe they came from Asia. Others feel they had always lived in Italy. It is apparent the Etruscans were influenced by the Greeks. The major Etruscan gods were similar to those of Greece. The Etruscan **alphabet** is based on the Greek alphabet. The Etruscans even decorated their tombs with scenes from Greek mythology. The Etruscans passed much of their culture to the Romans.

Etruscan warrior 500 B.C.

Etruscan Trade

Etruria was wealthy because of its fertile land and rich mineral ore resources. Etruscans traded with the Greeks, Phoenicians, and with people as far away as France, Spain, and Africa. They had exceptional harbors that promoted trade, but most Etruscan cities were several miles inland from the ocean. This protected them from piracy.

Etruscan Government

The Etruscans were more advanced than the Romans in the seventh century B.C. They conquered Rome and ruled them for about 100 years. However, they had no strong central government. Instead there were a number of city-states. The Etruscans formed a league of 12 cities; each was ruled by a priest-king called a **lucomon**. The lucomon was elected each year and was selected from the nobility that governed each city.

Etruscan Cities

The Etruscans were excellent **engineers**. Their cities were well planned with bridges, canals, and temples. They had paved streets and brick houses. The cities were often surrounded by walls for protection. The streets were well drained and designed to bear heavy traffic. Rome had a drain and a pattern of underground water tunnels throughout the city.

The Roman Republic Takes Over

By the third century B.C., the Romans had become more powerful, and the Etruscan Civilization was absorbed by the Roman Republic. The Etruscan culture gradually disappeared, although their language did continue to be used for some religious ceremonies. The Romans were influenced by Etruscan art, architecture, and religion. The Etruscans also gave the Romans the alphabet, writing, and many different crafts.

ETRUSCAN EMPIRE AT A GLANCE

WHERE: Central Italy in what is now called Tuscany

WHEN: 800 B.C.–300 B.C.

ACHIEVEMENTS:
- Cities were well planned with paved streets and brick houses
- Skilled craftsmen
- Women had more freedom than the women in Greece or Rome
- Excellent sailors
- Built drains and underground water tunnels to remove excess water

---

Name: _____ Date: _____

Knowledge Check

Matching

_____ 1. Etruscans
_____ 2. Etruria
_____ 3. Tuscany
_____ 4. alphabet
_____ 5. lucomon
_____ 6. engineer

a. region in central Italy where the Etruscans lived

b. a writing system where each symbol stands for a sound

c. a priest-king who ruled an Etruscan city-state; selected from the nobility of the city

d. ancient people who lived in central Italy and were in power from about 800 to 300 B.C.

e. modern region of Italy from the Tiber River to the Arno River where the Etruscans once lived

f. a person who uses science, math, and planning to design and build things that are useful for others

Multiple Choice

7. Who influenced the Etruscans, especially with their gods and alphabet?
   a. the Tuscans
   b. the Greeks
   c. the Romans
   d. the Spanish

8. What did Etruscan cities avoid by building several miles inland from the ocean?
   a. pirates
   b. trade
   c. harbors
   d. drowning

9. Who absorbed and adopted much of the Etruscan culture, including their art, architecture, religion, alphabet, and writing?
   a. the Phoenicians
   b. the Greeks
   c. the Romans
   d. the French

Constructed Response

10. The Etruscans did not have a typical empire. Describe the kind of government they had. Use details from the reading selection to help support your answer.

_____
_____
_____
_____
_____
_____

The Celts

The **Celts** were people of Indo-European stock who first appeared in Central Europe in the eighth century B.C. They lived in the countries we now call Austria, the Czech Republic, Slovakia, Germany, Hungary, and Switzerland. They were the first people in Northern Europe to make **iron**. Iron tools made it possible for these early Celts to clear and farm more land than ever before. This allowed for growing more food, which resulted in an increased population and overcrowding. The Celts then spread to France, Belgium, Portugal, Spain, and the British Isles. Some Celtic groups moved to what are now Bulgaria and Greece. Some even settled in Northern Italy.

Classes in Celtic Society

By 500 B.C., the Celts had developed into a civilization. However, the Celts were not united under one leader. Their culture was divided into independent tribes. Within each tribe, the Celts were split into three classes. There were the nobles or aristocrats, which included warriors; the **Druids**, the priests or learned class, who were also noblemen; and the peasants or common people, which included farmers and craftsmen. Although these are the general groups within a Celtic tribe, members of one group would sometimes perform the functions of another.

Skilled Artisans and Workers

The Celts were some of the most skillful artisans of their time. They created intricate gold and metal works valued throughout the civilized world. They primarily used local materials to make pottery, enamel work, and jewelry. They were excellent farmers, herders, weavers, miners, and traders. They were also skilled road builders, which allowed them to expand into other countries.

The Two Sides of the Celts

Celts were a puzzle to those from other civilizations. They were ruthless warriors who often went into battle naked to show they were unafraid. They raided and looted, sacrificed humans, took slaves, and killed their enemies and collected their skulls. However, they were kind to those who were not their enemies. There is evidence that in 300 B.C. some tribes had built and ran a **hospital** to care for those who could not care for themselves.

Celtic parade helmet, 350 B.C.

Oral History

The artistic and musical Celts had no written language. Their history and literature was memorized and passed down **orally** from generation to generation. The Druids preserved this knowledge and served as teachers, judges, and doctors.

Clashes With the Romans

The Romans called the Celts Gauls and considered them a race of barbarians. The Romans wanted the land the Celts controlled. About 390 B.C., the armies of the Celts and the Romans clashed, and the Celts won a decisive victory. The Celts went to Rome and looted it. The Celtic victory was short-lived, however. For the next several centuries, the Romans conquered most of Europe. Today, only traces of the Celtic culture remain in the British Isles and in northwest France.

> **CELTIC CIVILIZATION AT A GLANCE**
> **WHERE:** Europe
> **WHEN:** 800 B.C. TO A.D. 200
> **ACHIEVEMENTS:**
> - Skillful artisans, artists, musicians
> - Excellent farmers
> - Fearless warriors
> - Built roads to expand into other countries
> - First people in Northern Europe to make iron

Name: _____ Date: _____

Knowledge Check

Matching

_____ 1. Celts

_____ 2. iron

_____ 3. Druids

_____ 4. hospital

_____ 5. orally

a. a place to care for those who could not care for themselves

b. people of Indo-European stock who first appeared in Central Europe and moved into Western Europe and the British Isles

c. a strong metal that can be extracted from certain kinds of rocks and made into tools and building materials

d. through the spoken word; by word of mouth

e. the priests or learned class of the Celts; served as teachers, judges, and doctors

Multiple Choice

6. What allowed the Celts to clear and farm more land, grow more food, and increase in population?
   a. fertile soil
   b. building roads
   c. raiding and looting
   d. iron tools

7. How did the Celts sometimes fight in battle?
   a. naked
   b. in armor
   c. in helmets
   d. with guns

8. Where can traces of the Celtic culture be found today?
   a. Rome
   b. the British Isles
   c. Austria
   d. Greece

9. What was one of the things that allowed the Celts to expand into other countries?
   a. a written language
   b. roads
   c. intricate gold work
   d. hospitals

Constructed Response

10. Describe how the Celts passed down their history and literature. Use details from the reading selection to help support your answer.

_____

_____

_____

_____

_____

_____

Ancient Rome

The Founding of Rome

Like the Greeks, Romans had myths, legends, and gods they used to explain the world, their history, and their heritage. One famous Roman legend explains how Rome was founded. According

to the story, Rome was founded by **Romulus** and **Remus**, twin brothers who were the sons of Mars, the Roman god of war. Shortly after birth, a wicked relative tried to drown the twins by throwing them into the Tiber River. They were washed ashore, and a female wolf rescued them and fed them as if they were her own. The boys were found and raised by a shepherd and his wife. When the boys grew up, they founded Rome and then quarreled over who would be king. Romulus killed Remus and became the first of Rome's seven kings, reigning from 753 to 716 B.C.

Roman history can be divided into three periods: the Monarchy, the Republic, and the Empire.

THE MONARCHY

Rome was first ruled by kings, sometimes called **monarchs**. The city was governed by six kings after Romulus. During this period, the city grew, the Roman religion was established, and roads, aqueducts, and bridges were built. The last of the seven kings of this period was Tarquinius the Proud, a tyrant who was so hated, he was thrown out in 509 B.C. After Tarquinius was thrown out, the wealthy landowners in Rome established a Republic.

THE ROMAN REPUBLIC

A **republic** is a political system in which a group of citizens elects representatives and officers to run the government. A republic is sometimes a democracy. However, the one established in Rome was not a democracy because only people from powerful, wealthy families belonged to the senate. The **senate** was the assembly of aristocrats who elected or appointed many people to perform public jobs. The two most important people they appointed were called **consuls**. The consuls were given a great deal of authority to make decisions for Rome. When Rome had an extreme emergency, the senate could appoint a **dictator** to deal with the crisis.

Roman Social Classes

The wealthy class in Rome was known as the **patricians**. **Plebeians** were the common people in Rome. They were the traders, workers, and peasants. While the Republic worked well for

---

ROMAN EMPIRE AT A GLANCE

WHERE: Italy

WHEN: 500 B.C.–A.D. 1453

ACHIEVEMENTS:

- United many people and established peace over a great area
- Established laws that served as a basis for legal systems for many countries
- Latin, its language, is the basis for many other languages such as Italian, French, Portuguese, and Spanish.
- Built magnificent structures such as the Colosseum and the Pantheon; their architects made extensive use of the dome and arch
- Built paved roads, bridges, and aqueducts to carry water
- Invented the numbering system called Roman numerals, which is still used
- Developed the Julian calendar, which is still used today
- Introduced concrete and road signs

---

the patricians, who were able to make decisions in the senate, the plebeians felt they were no better off, since they could not hold office and had no voice in the government. The friction caused by this inequity continued until 493 B.C. when the plebeians were given representatives, called **tribunes**, in the senate. The plebeians were able to have the tribunes establish a set of protective laws.

Hannibal crossing the Alps during the Second Punic War

Wars

In addition to the conflict between the patricians and the plebeians, the Roman Republic also had to deal with a series of wars with its neighbors. Fortunately, Rome had a large, strong army, a plentiful food supply, metals to make weapons, and slaves to do much of the work. Each war brought new power and new land under Roman domination. Eventually, the Romans controlled all of Italy and most of the land facing the Mediterranean Sea. Greece, part of Spain, and Gaul, now known as France, were all under Roman control. The main enemy of Rome was Carthage in North Africa. Rome and Carthage fought three wars called the **Punic Wars** over a hundred-year period.

Roman Provinces

Each new land acquired by the Romans became a **province**. The Romans signed a treaty with each defeated nation requiring them to pay taxes to Rome. In exchange, the important people of the conquered nation could become Roman citizens, vote in elections, and become elected to public office. Those who chose to become Roman citizens had to adopt a Roman name and wear Roman clothes. Even the conquered people who did not become citizens often adopted the Roman language and its customs.

THE ROMAN EMPIRE

Continued military victories made some Roman generals very powerful. Soldiers began to give their loyalty to the generals rather than to the senate or Rome. Some generals used this loyalty to try to become dictators and take power away from the senate. There was chaos in Rome. No one was able to stay in power for very long. In 46 B.C. **Julius Caesar**, a general and hero, became dictator.

Julius Ceasar

Julius Caesar

Caesar accomplished many things in the short time he was dictator. He reduced taxes, built buildings, and reformed the calendar. The Julian calendar was named after him, and although there have been a few minor changes, it is still used today. The changes Caesar made in Rome improved the lives of the plebeians, so they liked him. His soldiers liked him too. However, the patricians did not like him because he had become too powerful. Several senators decided to kill him, and on March 15, 44 B.C., Caesar was assassinated.

Rome's Golden Age

Eventually, Caesar's adopted son, Octavian, assumed power and became the first **emperor** of Rome. He called himself **Augustus**, which means "great." This was the beginning of the Roman Empire. It is sometimes called the Age of Emperors or Rome's Golden Age. While consuls were still elected every year, the emperor was the absolute ruler.

Map of the Roman Empire A.D. 284

Augustus was a good ruler. He kept peace, built roads and buildings, and encouraged the arts and sciences. He ruled from 27 B.C. until A.D. 14. After Augustus, there were other emperors, some better than others. There was peace, however, and the empire continued to grow. Although there were occasional rebellions against Roman rule, those conquered came to accept being part of the Roman Empire. In A.D. 212, the Emperor Caracalle decreed that all free men and women, including those who had previously been slaves, were Roman citizens. Slaves could not claim citizenship.

Augustus

The Decline and Fall of the Roman Empire

About A.D. 180, the Roman Empire began to decline. The Empire was so large that it was hard to manage. It was divided into two parts—the **Latin Western Empire** and the **Greek Eastern Empire**. Rome remained the capital of the Western Empire. The Greek Eastern Empire was also called the **Byzantine Empire**. Constantinople was the capital of the Greek Eastern Empire. It was named after the Emperor Constantine. The Western Empire was invaded by various Germanic tribes and by Mongols called Huns. It fell in A.D. 476. The Eastern Empire was toppled in 1453 when the Turks conquered Constantinople. The Romans called all these invaders **barbarians**, which meant they lived outside the empire. The fall of ancient Rome was complete. But many of its buildings, ideas of government, and remnants of its language exist today.

Name: _____ Date: _____

Knowledge Check

Matching

_____ 1. monarch

_____ 2. senate

_____ 3. consuls

_____ 4. dictator

_____ 5. patricians

_____ 6. plebeians

_____ 7. tribunes

_____ 8. province

_____ 9. barbarians

a. invaders who lived outside the Roman Empire

b. the common people of Rome

c. two men given authority to make decisions for the Roman Republic

d. a ruler such as a king

e. someone the senate appointed to deal with a crisis

f. the wealthy class in Rome

g. new land acquired by the Romans

h. the assembly of aristocrats who elected or appointed people to perform public jobs

i. representatives of the common people in the Roman senate

Multiple Choice

10. Which legendary brother founded Rome and became its first king?
    a. Romulus
    b. Remus
    c. Caesar
    d. Augustus

11. Which man was once called Octavian and became the first emperor of Rome?
    a. Romulus
    b. Remus
    c. Caesar
    d. Augustus

12. Which part of the Roman world was the last to fall?
    a. the Monarchy
    b. the Latin Western Empire
    c. the Greek Eastern Empire
    d. the Republic

Constructed Response

13. Explain what happened to new lands acquired by the Romans. Use details from the reading selection to help support your answer.

_____

_____

_____

_____

_____

_____

_____

_____

Name: _____ Date: _____

Explore: The Julian Calendar

The Romans used various calendars based on the sun, moon, and seasons. These calendars were also influenced by political and religious considerations, so they were not very accurate. When Julius Caesar became dictator, the Roman calendar was in error by several months. Caesar asked Sosigenes, the astronomer, to help him reform the calendar so that it was accurate. Sosigenes created a calendar of 365 days and 6 hours. In order to make up for past errors so that the calendar would correspond with the seasons, the year 46 B.C. was given 445 days. After that, every year was to be based on the solar year, which is approximately 365 days and 6 hours. There were some changes later, but basically this Julian calendar is still in use today.

You may have wondered how the months of the year got their names. The name for each month has its roots in Rome. You should understand that the earliest Latin calendar had ten months, beginning with March. The 12-month calendar was developed during the reign of Julius Caesar. That is why it is called the Julian calendar.

Shown below are the root words for the months. They are not in any particular order. In the blank, write the modern name of the month taken from the Roman word.

ROOT WORD	MONTH
1. *Novem*, which means *nine*	_____
2. *Octo*, which means *eight*	_____
3. *Februare*, which means *to clean*	_____
4. *Decem,* which means *ten*	_____
5. *Augustus Caesar*, the Roman Emperor	_____
6. *Juno*, the Roman goddess	_____
7. *Mars*, the Roman god of war	_____
8. *Julius Caesar*, the Roman dictator	_____
9. *Janus*, the Roman god who was the doorkeeper of heaven	_____
10. *Septem*, which means *seven*	_____
11. *Maia*, the Roman goddess of spring	_____
12. *Aperire*, which means *to open*	_____

The Vikings

"The Vikings are coming! The Vikings are coming!" This is the dreaded alarm that spread terror throughout Europe from the late eighth to the 11th century A.D. The Vikings attacked and raided cities all across Europe, including London and Paris. **Monasteries** were the frequent targets of raids because that was often where a region's wealth was stored. The Vikings would raid a monastery, steal its treasures, kidnap the monks, and sell them as slaves in the East.

Swift Raids

The key to the success of the Viking raids was surprise and swiftness. They often planned their attacks for Sunday, when they knew the people and the monks would be in church. Their longships were very shallow, making it possible for them to sail right onto the beach or inland into the rivers, quickly get off their ship, raid the monastery, put their loot on the ship, and escape before the people could mount an organized defense.

Viking History Told in Sagas

The **Vikings**, which is a word that means "pirates," were not all ruthless, plundering soldiers. In fact, until the end of the eighth century, most Vikings lived peacefully. Originally known as Norsemen or Danes, the Vikings were hunters, farmers, fishermen, and craftsmen living in the **Scandinavian** countries we now call Norway, Denmark, and Sweden. They were excellent seamen, navigators, craftsmen, shipbuilders, traders, and great storytellers. We know a great deal of their history through stories of their adventures that are called **sagas**. As the Viking population grew, the scarcity of land caused many Vikings to leave their homes and become seamen and soldiers. Some explored other lands and established settlements in places like Greenland, Iceland, England, Scotland, Spain, France, and Ireland. Some sailed into the Mediterranean, and others traveled to what is now America, centuries before Columbus. Others chose to raid towns and monasteries for treasures, food, and slaves.

A Berserker

Berserkers

The Vikings had a fierce reputation. In fact, the word *berserk* comes from the Viking word *berserkr,* which meant "bear-shirt." A **berserker** was a brave warrior who would put on a bear skin prior to a battle and work himself into a frenzy to prepare for the fight. It is said that a berserker was a madman in battle. It was a great honor for a Viking to die in battle. Those who did were transported to Valhalla. The Vikings believed **Valhalla** was a paradise where the dead would enjoy themselves by fighting and feasting.

Shipbuilding and Sailing

Perhaps the skills that made the Vikings unique were shipbuilding and sailing. While other Europeans kept close to shore when they sailed, Vikings crossed the Atlantic Ocean without a compass or other modern instruments. Archaeologists believe they were able to navigate these great distances by observing the sun, stars, and the different species of birds and sea animals they would see. They even tasted sea water as they were sailing. If the water was less salty, they knew that land was close by, since fresh water empties into the ocean.

A Viking Longship

The Vikings had different sizes of ships. One kind only held four men, while fighting ships, called **longships**, were up to 90 feet long and held 50 warriors. All ships were designed in a similar manner. They were long, thin, and light with a curve at each end. They were flexible so they wouldn't break up on the rough ocean. A large, square sail moved the ship when the wind was strong enough. When it wasn't, the men rowed. In bad weather, the sail was lowered and used as a tent to protect the sailors.

Their ships could sail inland on rivers. They had a keel that cut through the water quickly and made the ship stable. The prow of a longship was carved into a menacing figure, such as a dragon or snake. They were very fast, and their rudders made them easy to maneuver.

A great deal of the Vikings' culture involved their ships. Not only were they important for raids, trading, and moving to new settlements, many rich Vikings were either buried or cremated in ships. These ships were stuffed with items the deceased might need on their journey to the next world. Ordinary people were sometimes buried in graves marked with stones in the shape of a ship.

Viking Religion

The Vikings believed there were many gods who lived in **Asgard**. The main god was Odin or Wodan, the ruler of Valhalla. Valhalla was a hall in Asgard where dead warriors were brought back to life. Odin's son was Thor, the god of thunder and of law and order. Thor would throw his hammer at monsters and drive his chariot pulled by goats across the sky, thus making the noise of thunder. Freya was a fertility goddess, and Tiu was a god of war.

Social Classes

The Vikings had three different classes of people—aristocrats, freemen, and slaves. The aristocrats were nobles and were called **jarls**. They owned land, ships, and slaves. A jarl could eventually become a king of his region. Freemen were **karls**. They were free-born peasants and often owned land. Some were traders, craftsmen, or worked on farms owned by others. The slaves were **thralls**. They were prisoners of war or children whose parents were thralls. All freemen attended

Asgard

open-air meetings called **things** to discuss problems and settle disputes.

Days of the Week

The Viking influence is still with us today. Shown below are the origins of the days of the week. Many are taken from the Norse language.

Sunday: Day of the sun (Germanic)
Monday: Day of the moon (Germanic)
Tuesday: Day of Tiu or Tyr, the Norse god of war
Wednesday: Day of Odin or Woden, the chief Norse god
Thursday: Day of Thor, the Norse god of thunder
Friday: Day of Freya, the Norse goddess of love
Saturday: Day of Saturn, the Roman god Saturn

Name: _____ Date: _____

Knowledge Check

Matching

_____ 1. monasteries   a. stories of Viking adventures

_____ 2. Vikings   b. freemen; free-born peasants

_____ 3. sagas   c. fighting ships up to 90 feet long and holding 50 warriors

_____ 4. berserker   d. places where religious men called monks lived and worked

_____ 5. longships   e. aristocrats; nobles

_____ 6. jarls   f. slaves

_____ 7. karls   g. a brave warrior who wore a bear skin and worked himself into

_____ 8. thralls   a frenzy to prepare for a fight

                           h. from a word that means "pirates"; Norsemen who came from

                           Scandinavia and were feared as fierce raiders

Multiple Choice

9. Where did the Vikings believe the gods lived?

     a. Scandinavia   b. Valhalla

     c. Asgard   d. monasteries

10. Where were rich Vikings often buried?

     a. in a tomb   b. in a ship

     c. in a pyramid   d. in a cave

11. All freemen could go to these open-air meetings to discuss problems and settle disputes.

     a. things   b. sagas

     c. berserkers   d. jarls

Constructed Response

12. Why did the Vikings especially want to raid monasteries? Use details from the reading selection to help support your answer.

_____

_____

_____

_____

_____

_____

_____

_____

The Middle East: The Phoenicians

The **Phoenicians** lived in small independent city-states along the Mediterranean coast in what is now Lebanon from about 2000 B.C. to 800 B.C. Two famous Phoenician cities are Tyre and Sidon. The people were originally Canaanites, but the Greeks named them Phoenicians. It is thought the name Phoenician comes from the Greek word ***phoinikes***, meaning "purple men." The Greeks gave them that name because the Phoenicians developed the process of making purple dye. It was so expensive that only the wealthy could afford it. Roman emperors wore purple togas, and over time, the color purple became associated with royalty.

Phoenician Trade Goods

Other Phoenician products were also prized throughout the Mediterranean. Fine glassware was made into vases, bottles, goblets, and beads. The Phoenicians learned glassmaking from the Egyptians, but they improved the process. The Phoenicians used sand rich in **quartz** from their own country, making the glass clear instead of cloudy. Both clear and colored glassware made by Phoenician craftsmen were treasured objects. Beautiful ivory and wood carvings, pottery, cedar wood, wine, wrought metal objects, and embroidered cloth also made Phoenician traders wealthy.

Sailors and Navigators

By 1250 B.C., the Phoenicians had also established themselves as outstanding navigators and sailors. Their skills were developed by sailing all over the Mediterranean world, looking for new markets and raw materials for their products. According to a Greek historian, they may have even sailed around Africa, about 2,000 years before Europeans accomplished this feat. Phoenicians were among the first people to learn to sail at night by navigating by the stars.

A Phoenician Ship

Trading Posts

The Phoenicians set up trading posts in many places in the Mediterranean. The most famous trading post was in **Carthage** in northern Africa, which became a power in the Mediterranean by the seventh century B.C. There were other important trading posts at Utica near Carthage, Cadiz in southern Spain, and on the islands of Cyprus and Rhodes.

The Alphabet

Perhaps the greatest accomplishment of the Phoenicians was the invention of the alphabet. Earlier civilizations had developed forms of writing based on pictures called **pictographs**. In the Phoenician **alphabet**, each symbol represented a sound. Since there are about 30 different sounds in speech, this means that words can be written using a system of 30 letters or less. The Phoenicians used 22 letters. The Greeks adapted the Phoenician letters and called the first letter "alpha" and the second letter "beta." Combining these two letters gives us the word "alphabet." Today all modern European languages are written with the alphabetic system.

> **PHOENICIAN CIVILIZATION AT A GLANCE**
> **WHERE:** West Asia
> **WHEN:** 2000 B.C.–800 B.C.
> **ACHIEVEMENTS:**
> - Invented the alphabet and a writing system; most early writing systems were based on pictures
> - The greatest traders of the ancient world
> - Talented craftsmen known for their ivory carvings
> - Developed the technique of glassblowing
> - Excellent navigators, sailors, and shipbuilders.

Name: _____ Date: _____

Knowledge Check

Matching

_____ 1. Phoenicians

_____ 2. phoinikes

_____ 3. quartz

_____ 4. Carthage

_____ 5. pictographs

_____ 6. alphabet

a. the most famous Phoenician trading post; located in northern Africa

b. a six-sided crystalline mineral that may be present in the sand used to produce glass

c. Greek word meaning "purple men"

d. pictures that stand for words

e. traders and seafaring people who lived along the Mediterranean coast in what is now Lebanon

f. a writing system using symbols that stand for different sounds in speech

Multiple Choice

7. Who was most likely to wear purple clothing in ancient times?

   a. sailors
         b. teachers

   c. emperors
      d. craftsmen

8. The Phoenicians improved upon the glassmaking skills they learned from what civilization?

   a. Egyptians
      b. Sumerians

   c. Greeks
        d. Romans

9. How many letters were in the Phoenician alphabet?

   a. 20
     b. 22
     c. 26
     d. 30

10. What was one of the main Phoenician cities in the area that is now Lebanon?

   a. Cadiz
      b. Carthage

   c. Tyre
       d. Utica

Constructed Response

11. Describe how the Phoenicians gained their sailing and navigating skills and how much territory they covered. Use details from the reading selection to help support your answer.

_____

_____

_____

_____

_____

_____

_____

The Hebrews

The **Hebrews** were a nomadic group of **Semitic** people who originally came from Mesopotamia about 2000 B.C. and settled in an area close to the Mediterranean Sea in the Middle East. Most of the migration occurred between the 14th and 12th centuries B.C. Hebrews, the ancestors of today's Jews, called the area where they settled **Israel**.

The Exodus

Some of the Hebrews moved to Egypt in search of more fertile land. Eventually, the pharoahs of Egypt made the Israelites slaves. **Moses**, who was of Hebrew descent but lived as an Egyptian for part of his life, finally got the Israelites released from their bondage. Moses led the Hebrews out of Egypt and on a journey through the wilderness. Their escape from Egypt is known as the **Exodus**, which means "to leave." Joshua, Moses' successor, led the Hebrews as they conquered Canaan and made **Jerusalem** their capital.

Hebrew Religion

An important element of the Hebrew culture was its religion. Hebrews developed the idea of **monotheism**, which means they believed there was only one god. Most other cultures believed the world was created and ruled by many gods; this philosophy is called **polytheism**. The Hebrews believed that the God who created the world also controlled the world. They believed that people could talk to God through prayer. They also believed that the image of God should not be made into a statue and worshipped. Many of these beliefs were radical at the time.

The Twelve Tribes of Israel

Hebrew Laws

Their laws also set the Hebrews apart. In most cultures, the king or a group of nobles made strict laws for governing the common people. Often, the kings and noblemen did not obey the laws. The Hebrews, however, had a set of laws based on their religion, and they applied them to everyone, including the rulers. Some of their laws, called the "Ten Commandments," are found in the Jewish scriptures called the *Torah*. They are also found in Exodus in the Old Testament of the Christian *Bible*.

HEBREW CIVILIZATION AT A GLANCE

WHERE: The Middle East

WHEN: 2000 B.C.–30 B.C.

ACHIEVEMENTS:

- Believed in one god
- Established a set of moral laws called the "Ten Commandments"
- Their religious beliefs strongly influenced many modern-day religions
- Recorded their history, laws, and beliefs in the Torah and Old Testament

---

Hebrew History

The Hebrew tribes rose to power led by kings Saul, David, and Solomon. The kingdom eventually split into two small states, Israel and Judah, but these states were eventually destroyed. Israel was conquered by Assyria in 721 B.C. Judah was conquered by Babylonia in 587 B.C. This region has been controlled by several foreign powers, including the Persians, Alexander the Great, the Hellenistic Ptolemies, and the Romans.

World Religions Develop in Jerusalem

Three major religions developed in Jerusalem. They are **Judaism**, which is the Jewish religion; **Christianity**, developed by the followers of Jesus Christ; and **Islam**, which is followed in the Muslim world.

Name: _____ Date: _____

Knowledge Check

Matching

_____ 1. Hebrews
_____ 2. Semitic
_____ 3. Exodus
_____ 4. monotheism
_____ 5. polytheism
_____ 6. Judaism
_____ 7. Christianity
_____ 8. Islam

a. the Hebrews' escape from Egypt; means "to leave"
b. religion followed in the Muslim world
c. believing in only one god
d. a nomadic group of Semitic people who settled near the Mediterranean Sea; ancestors of today's Jews
e. the Jewish religion
f. the language family that includes Hebrew, Aramaic, and Arabic
g. believing in many gods
h. religion developed by the followers of Jesus Christ

Multiple Choice

9. What were the two kingdoms into which the Hebrews split? (Circle two.)
   a. Assyria
   b. Babylon
   c. Israel
   d. Judah

10. What is the name of the Jewish scriptures where their laws are found?
    a. the Bible
    b. the Torah
    c. the Law
    d. the Psalms

11. What was NOT part of the Hebrew religion?
    a. praying to God
    b. believing in one god
    c. following the Ten Commandments
    d. worshipping statues of God

Critical Thinking

12. Why do you think laws based on religion might have worked better than laws declared by a king? Use details from the reading selection to help support your answer.

_____

_____

_____

_____

_____

_____

_____

_____

The Persians

The **Persian Empire** was located east of the Fertile Crescent on the east side of the Persian Gulf. It was one of the largest empires of the ancient world. Persia occupied land that is presently Iran and Afghanistan. Persians were not Semitic, as many of the early civilizations in that part of the world had been. They were Indo-European and called themselves **Aryans**. The name Iran is based on the name Aryan.

Cyrus the Great

Cyrus and the Persians Rise to Power

The Persians and the Medes came to this area about 1300 B.C. The **Medes** were warriors who raided cities and caravans. In 550 B.C., **Cyrus the Great**, a Persian province ruler, led an army to defeat the Medes. Cyrus united the Medes and the Persians into a strong army.

Cyrus and his army were very successful. In only 15 years, his army of archers and cavalrymen conquered almost all of the ancient world. This included Asia Minor, the Fertile Crescent, the Indus Valley, and Egypt. The Persians treated those they defeated fairly and kindly. In fact, there is some evidence that when the Babylonians were defeated by the Persians, many Babylonians welcomed the Persians because they were unhappy with their own king. Cyrus freed the Jewish captives and led them back to Jerusalem. The Persians allowed the kingdoms they defeated to maintain their own cultures rather than making them adopt the Persian culture. Conquered people did, however, have to pay tribute to Persia. Cyrus was killed in battle in 530 B.C.

Managing the Persian Empire

The Persian Empire gained prominence under the leadership of Darius I, who ruled from 522 to 486 B.C. Darius was a very good administrator and organizer. Since the Persian Empire was so large, the challenge was to maintain the lands it had acquired and to govern them. Darius divided this enormous empire into 20 provinces called **satrapies**. Each of these satrapies was managed by a governor called a **satrap**. Other leaders, such as judges and tax collectors, were Persians appointed by the emperor. The emperor also had an inspector who would visit the satrapies unannounced to make sure the officials were doing their jobs well and being loyal to the emperor. The Persians connected their empire with well-paved roads, which encouraged international trade.

Zoroastrianism

One contribution of the Persians was the religion called **Zoroastrianism**. **Zoroaster** was a Persian prophet who had seven visions. These visions were the basis for the religion. Zoroastrianism became the official religion of the Persian empire and flourished for many years. It is still practiced in some places today. The *Avesta*, the Persian holy book, based on the views of Zoroaster, teaches that there is one supreme god who was the god of life and created everything that is good in the world. Another god created everything that was evil and bad. He was the god of death.

> **PERSIAN CIVILIZATION AT A GLANCE**
> **WHERE:** East of the Fertile Crescent in the Middle East
> **WHEN:** 550 B.C.–330 B.C.
> **ACHIEVEMENTS:**
> - Built roads and canals
> - Divided the empire into provinces so that it could be governed better
> - Wrote the *Avesta,* the Persian holy book, based on the views of Zoroaster, a prophet
> - Did not invent coinage, but were the first to put it to wide use

The Persian Empire Ends

Persia fought several wars with the Greeks. The Persian Empire lasted until 330 B.C. when it was conquered by Alexander the Great.

Name: _____ Date: _____

Knowledge Check

Matching

_____ 1. Aryans

_____ 2. Medes

_____ 3. satrapies

_____ 4. satrap

_____ 5. Zoroastriansim

_____ 6. Zoroaster

_____ 7. Avesta

a. a governor of a Persian province

b. warriors who raided cities and caravans and settled in the same area as the Persians

c. a Persian prophet who had seven visions

d. the 20 provinces into which Darius divided the Persian empire

e. what the Persians called themselves

f. the Persian holy book, based on the views of Zoroaster

g. religion founded by Zoroaster based on his seven visions

Multiple Choice

8. Which Persian ruler united the Persians and the Medes into a strong army?

    a. Cyrus

    b. Darius

    c. Xerxes

    d. Alexander

9. What did conquered people in the Persian Empire have to do?

    a. worship Cyrus as a god

    b. pay tribute to Persia

    c. adopt the Persian culture

    d. work as slaves for the Persians

10. What was one thing that encouraged international trade in the Persian Empire?

    a. inspectors

    b. Zoroastrianism

    c. a strong army

    d. well-paved roads

Constructed Response

11. Why were some Babylonians happy to be conquered by the Persians? Use details from the reading selection to help support your answer.

_____

_____

_____

_____

_____

_____

_____

Name: _____ Date: _____

Map Follow-Up

On the map of the Persian Empire shown below, find and label:

The Mediterranean Sea   **The Black Sea**   **The Red Sea**
The Caspian Sea   **The Persian Gulf**   **The Arabian Sea**
The Sahara Desert   **Crete**   **Cyprus**

The Persian Empire

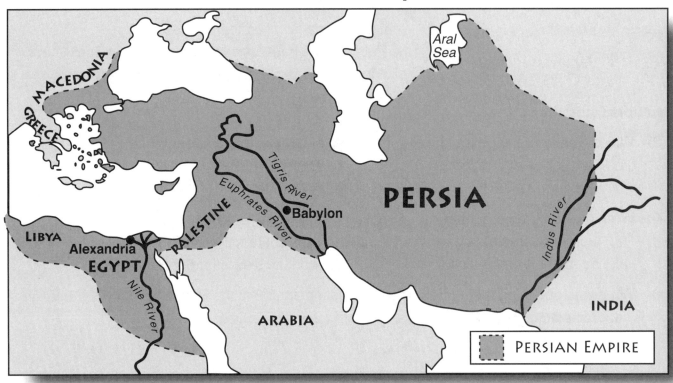

Write a paragraph describing the difficulties involved in ruling a large empire, such as the Persian Empire.

_____

_____

_____

_____

_____

_____

_____

_____

The Byzantine Empire

The Roman Empire Split in Two

The Roman Empire was so large that it was hard to manage, so in A.D. 284 it was divided in two. The section in the west was called the Latin Western Empire, and the section in the east was called the Greek Eastern Empire. The Greek Eastern Empire was also called the **Byzantine Empire**. The center of the Greek Eastern part of the Roman Empire was the old Greek city of **Byzantium**. It lies on both sides of the **Bosporus**, a narrow strait of water between Europe and Asia. Byzantium was a valuable port strategically located for trade and military purposes. It controlled the sea route between the Black Sea and the Mediterranean and the trade routes from Europe to the East. Byzantium was rebuilt as a capital city by Emperor **Constantine the Great**. It was then renamed **Constantinople** after the emperor. Constantinople, called Istanbul today, flourished and became as splendid as Rome.

Constantine the Great

The Spread of Christianity

In the second and third centuries A.D., Christianity was spreading throughout the Roman Empire, even though Christians were persecuted and put to death for their religion. In Byzantium, however, things changed. Constantine became a Christian after he had a vision. He issued an order that allowed others to worship as Christians. He eventually encouraged the spread of Christianity, which was important for the development of the Byzantine Empire. Gradually, Christianity became the official religion of the empire, as well as for medieval western Europe.

Culture of the Eastern Roman Empire

The word *Byzantium* refers to both the state and the culture of the Eastern Roman Empire during the Middle Ages. In 476, the Latin Western Empire was conquered by Germanic invaders. What was left of the Roman Empire was now ruled from Constantinople. In the sixth century, the Byzantine Empire stretched from southern Spain in the West to the borders of Sassanian Iran in the East. The Byzantine Empire was a diverse culture that combined many ethnic groups, languages, religions, and creeds. The Byzantines considered themselves Romans and faithfully maintained many of the traditions of Rome and Greece. When the Arabs conquered Egypt and Syria in 634, Byzantium changed. It became more Greek and less Roman. The Romans living in the Latin Western part of the Roman Empire did not regard those living in the Greek Eastern part very highly.

Byzantine Art and Architecture

Byzantium was known for its art. Art created during this period is called Byzantine. Architecture, mosaics, enamel work, ivory carving, and metal work were all forms of art that developed in new and distinctive ways. Many of the works of art were created for altars of churches and

> **BYZANTINE CIVILIZATION AT A GLANCE**
>
> **WHERE:** Europe—The eastern section of the Roman Empire
>
> **WHEN:** A.D. 284–1450
>
> **ACHIEVEMENTS:**
> - Preserved Greek and Roman culture and law
> - Produced great works of art including architecture, mosaics, enamel work, ivory carving, and metal work
> - Lasted over 1,000 years
> - Spread of Christianity

The Siege of Constantinople in 1453

imperial courts. One of the great architectural achievements of Byzantium was the construction of the church of **Hagia Sophia**, also known as Saint Sophia. It was built in Constantinople between A.D. 532 and 537. Today it is a mosque used by Muslims.

The Ottomans Conquer Byzantium

When the Ottomans came to power by the end of the sixth century, the Empire was being squeezed from all sides. The empire began to shrink as Arabs, Avars, Persians, Slavs, and Turks all conquered parts of Byzantium. By 1453, all that was left of the Byzantine Empire was Constantinople. In May of that year, the Ottoman Turks captured the city and changed the name of Constantinople to **Istanbul**. The loss of Constantinople to the Ottoman Empire was devastating to Western Europe. It was not only the end of Roman history and Christian power in the Eastern Mediterranean, it meant the Ottomans dominated trade through this important area.

The Byzantine Empire set a standard of cultural excellence for both halves of the Roman Empire. The cultural development of the Byzantine Empire has had a lasting impact on modern nations.

Name: _____ Date: _____

Knowledge Check

Matching

_____ 1. Byzantine Empire

_____ 2. Byzantium

_____ 3. Bosporus

_____ 4. Constantine the Great

_____ 5. Constantinople

_____ 6. Hagia Sophia

_____ 7. Istanbul

a. Roman emperor who rebuilt Byzantium as the capital of the eastern part of the Roman Empire

b. church built in Constantinople in 532–537

c. the first name of the capital of the Byzantine Empire; also the name of the culture of this empire

d. name given to the capital city by the Ottoman Turks

e. name of the capital city of the Greek Eastern Empire; named after a Roman emperor

f. a narrow strait of water between Europe and Asia

g. another name for the Greek Eastern part of the Roman Empire

Multiple Choice

8. After 634, Byzantium became much more like what culture?
   a. Roman
   b. Greek
   c. Arab
   d. Egyptian

9. Many pieces of Byzantine art were created for what?
   a. church altars
   b. museums
   c. public squares
   d. private homes

10. Who finally captured Constantinople in 1453?
    a. the Arabs
    b. the Persians
    c. the Ottoman Turks
    d. the Greeks

Constructed Response

11. Explain why Byzantium was in a valuable location for trade and military purposes. Use details from the reading selection to help support your answer.

_____

_____

_____

_____

_____

_____

The Muslim and Ottoman Empires

Islam

In the seventh century A.D., a prophet named **Muhammad** founded a new religion in Arabia. The people who lived in Arabia were called **Arabs**. This new religion was called **Islam**, and those who belonged to this religion were called **Muslims**. Islam means "surrender to the will of Allah." *Allah* is the Arabic name for God. The Muslims felt their religion was the only true religion and that it was their duty to tell everyone.

The Muslim Empire

Under the leadership of Muhammad, the **Muslim Empire** began to grow and take land from the Persian Empire and the Byzantine Empire. The first capital of the Muslim Empire was Damascus in Syria. Baghdad in Iraq later became its capital. Although Muhammad died in 632, the empire expanded, and by the eighth century, it extended from Spain to India. The Muslim rulers, called **caliphs**, did not force people to accept their faith, but those who did become Muslims paid lower taxes and were given other benefits. Many Christians and Jews refused to give up their own faith.

> ### MUSLIM AND OTTOMAN EMPIRES AT A GLANCE
> **WHERE:** The Near East, Balkans, Southern Russia, and Northern Africa
> **WHEN:** A.D. 800–1923
> **ACHIEVEMENTS:**
> - Built many libraries, mosques, and schools
> - Produced many great literary works
> - Advanced the study of mathematics
> - Developed and spread the Muslim religion
> - Performed surgery and used chemicals to make medicine

The Muslim Empire began to decline and was divided into several independent kingdoms. Eventually, the Turks, under their leader Seljuk, conquered most of the Near East. In 1258, the **Seljuk Turks** were defeated by the Mongols.

The Ottoman Empire

The Ottomans, who were related to the Turks, had originally been mercenary soldiers of the Seljuks. They took over the old Seljuk states and established a new Muslim Empire called the **Ottoman Empire**. The Ottoman Empire was named after their leader, Osman I. Osman's family ruled for almost 700 years. The empire was located in northwestern Anatolia near the Byzantine Empire.

The Ottomans felt it was their duty to defend their religion against those who were not Muslims. Osman, together with his son, Orkhan, conquered most of the Byzantine Empire by fighting a number of **jihads**, which are holy wars. Eventually, their empire expanded around Constantinople, but they were not able to capture Constantinople. Orkhan became sultan of the Ottoman Empire. *Sultan* is the Turkish name for "emperor." Constantinople was finally captured in 1453 by Mehmet II, who was called the Conqueror. He ordered the largest Christian church, the Hagia Sophia, to become a **mosque**, a place where Muslims worship.

Suleiman I

The Ottoman Empire reached its greatest power under Suleiman the Magnificent who ruled from 1520 to 1566. During his reign, the Ottomans conquered the Balkans, southern Russia, and northern Africa so that the empire now included much of eastern Europe and western Asia. Suleiman's accomplishments were not all military, however. He had mosques, monuments, bridges, roads, and schools built and also encouraged the arts and sciences.

The empire became weaker during the 18th and 19th centuries and came to an end after the First World War in 1923.

Name: _____ Date: _____

Knowledge Check

Matching

_____ 1. Muhammad

_____ 2. Arabs

_____ 3. Muslims

_____ 4. Islam

_____ 5. caliphs

_____ 6. Seljuk Turks

_____ 7. jihad

_____ 8. sultan

_____ 9. mosque

a. people who conquered most of the Near East part of the Muslim Empire and were eventually defeated by the Mongols

b. a place where Muslims worship

c. a holy war waged by Muslims, such as the Ottomans

d. people who live in Arabia

e. rulers of the Muslim Empire

f. Turkish word for the emperor of the Ottoman Empire

g. religion founded by Muhammad; means "surrrender to the will of Allah"

h. people who practice the Islamic religion

i. a prophet who founded the religion called Islam in Arabia

Multiple Choice

Seljuk Bey, leader of the Seljuk Turks

10. Which empire was named after its leader Osman I and conquered the Byzantine Empire, the Balkans, southern Russia, and northern Africa?

    a. the Arabian Empire   b. the Muslim Empire

    c. the Ottoman Empire   d. the Persian Empire

11. Which empire extended from Spain to India and was based on spreading the new religion founded by Muhammad?

    a. the Arabian Empire   b. the Muslim Empire

    c. the Ottoman Empire   d. the Persian Empire

Constructed Response

12. What happened in the Ottoman Empire during the reign of Suleiman the Magnificent? Use details from the reading selection to help support your answer.

_____

_____

_____

_____

_____

_____

_____

Name: _____ Date: _____

Explore: Three World Religions

There were three religions widely practiced during the time of the Ottoman Empire, and they are still practiced today. They are Judaism, Christianity, and Islam. These three monotheistic religions count about half the world's population as followers.

Listed below are statements that relate to either Judaism, Christianity, or Islam. Before each statement are the letters "J," which represents Judaism, "C," which represents Christianity, and "I," which represents Islam. Circle the letter to which the statement refers. Some statements may refer to more than one religion. You may have to do some research to find the answers.

J C I   1. Their holy book is called the *Koran*

J C I   2. The oldest religion of the three

J C I   3. Considers Jerusalem a holy city

J C I   4. Celebrates the holy month of Ramadan

J C I   5. The official religion of the Ottoman Empire

J C I   6. This religion was divided in the 16th century by the Reformation

J C I   7. The first religion to teach monotheism, or belief in one god

J C I   8. Place of worship is a church

J C I   9. Considers Jesus to be the Messiah promised by God in the Old Testament

J C I   10. Uses the term "kosher" to apply to food that may be eaten

J C I   11. Must pray five times a day

J C I   12. Awaits the second coming of Christ

J C I   13. The Sabbath is observed by refraining from work and by attending a synagogue

J C I   14. Place of worship is a mosque

J C I   15. Celebrates Christmas

J C I   16. Celebrates Passover

J C I   17. Place of worship is a synagogue

J C I   18. Must make a pilgrimage to Mecca at least once, if at all possible

J C I   19. Their holy book is called the *Bible*

J C I   20. Their holy book is called the *Torah*

J C I   21. Celebrates Easter

J C I   22. Worships Allah

J C I   23. Became the official religion of Rome in the fourth century

J C I   24. Recognizes Muhammad as the prophet of Allah

J C I   25. Abraham is considered a patriarch of this religion

Africa

KUSH

The Kush Pyramids at Meroe in Sudan

When one thinks of great civilizations or cultures in Africa, the name that leaps immediately to mind is Egypt. What many don't know is that there were other important civilizations that existed in Africa. This should not surprise anyone, since archaeologists claim the earliest humans lived in East Africa. Africa may well be the cradle of all humanity.

About 12,000 years ago, the area we now call the **Sahara Desert** was not a desert at all, but a fertile area. Lush vegetation extended across the continent. Within this rich area, humans lived who fished, hunted, and gathered. Eventually, they began to herd animals and farm. While the Egyptian culture flourished between 3100 B.C. and 332 B.C., civilizations to the south and to the west of Egypt were just beginning to develop. They were quite different from what most people think of as "civilization," nevertheless, the cultures that developed in Africa had music, art, and an oral history. They also traded gold, silver, copper, and ivory. One important African culture was known as the Kush.

The **Kush Civilization** was a very old civilization just south of Egypt along the Nile River. It was in an area we now call Sudan. The Kush Civilization began about 2000 B.C. and lasted until A.D. 350. The people of Kush were mainly fishermen and farmers. There were some tradesmen and some who built and sailed boats. The Egyptians were stronger than the Kush. They conquered them and took their precious metals, cattle, and ivory. They also enslaved them and took them back to Egypt. Eventually, the Kush grew stronger, and the Egyptians grew weaker. About 752 B.C. the Kush conquered the Egyptians, and for about a century, Kush kings governed Egypt.

The Kush ruled Egypt until they were conquered by the Assyrians who had iron weapons. Their defeat did not end the Kush civilization, however. They relocated their capital to Meroe and became a powerful culture. They mined and forged weapons and tools out of iron and spread their knowledge of iron-making to other parts of Africa. They developed a writing system, created art, and domesticated elephants. About A.D. 350, they were defeated by the Axum army.

GHANA

On the opposite side of the continent in West Africa, several kingdoms developed. The first of these West African empires was **Ghana**. Ghana was originally bordered on the west by the Senegal River, on the east by the Niger River, on the north by the Sahara Desert, and on the south by the jungle. It was this location that enabled Ghana to become rich and powerful. Although Ghana did not have as many resources as others in Africa, it was able to control the roads and charge taxes on **caravans** passing through the kingdom. The main items traded in this area were iron, gold, and salt.

AFRICAN EMPIRES AT A GLANCE

WHERE: Africa

WHEN: 2000 B.C. to present

ACHIEVEMENTS:
- Archaeological evidence shows this is where humans first lived.
- Kushites spread the knowledge of iron-making to other parts of Africa.
- Ghana controlled the gold and salt trade, established vital trade routes, and became wealthy by controlling trade routes and charging taxes.
- Zimbabweans were excellent builders who built a great walled city.

Ghana was a center for the iron industry. Its people made and traded iron weapons. Large numbers of warriors with iron weapons not only expanded the kingdom, but provided order to enable other tribes to trade and prosper. Although Ghana did have some gold, the area to the south of them had much more, and Ghana was able to control its trade. It is estimated that between the years A.D. 450 and 1230, more gold was traded in Ghana than at any other place in the world. While not as glamourous as gold, salt was also an important commodity in this era. Salt, which was mined in the Sahara Desert, was highly prized for its ability to preserve food.

The Ghana Kingdom became prominent around the eighth century, but flourished during the 10th and 11th centuries. Around 1200, when its kingdom extended from central Senegal to Timbuktu, Ghana's capital, Koumbi, was conquered by Berber Muslims. The kingdom of **Mali** followed the kingdom of Ghana. Mali included the area that once was Ghana, but it was larger.

ZIMBABWE

The city of Great Zimbabwe was located between the Zambezi and the Limpopo Rivers. **Zimbabwe**, which means "great stone houses," was settled by Bantu-speaking people in about the year A.D. 600. Those living in Zimbabwe mined gold and copper and began trading it with people in Asia. Between 950 and 1450, Zimbabwe became important as a religious center. It was trade, however, that created great wealth in the 12th century and enabled the Zimbabweans to begin a building period that lasted several centuries. While African buildings were usually made from mud-brick, **Great Zimbabwe** is an exception. A huge stone wall was constructed to enclose the city. Inside the city, other walls were built to separate one area from another.

While it took several centuries to build the wall surrounding the Great Zimbabwe, when it was finished, the structure was among the most impressive created during the iron age in Africa. The massive stone walls are spread over an area of about 60 acres. What makes them most remarkable is not only their size—they were sixteen feet thick at the bottom and were 35 feet high—but the fact that the granite bricks were cut and shaped so precisely that mortar or cement was not needed to hold them in place.

The City of Great Zimbabwe

The Great Zimbabwe enclosure was eventually abandoned, and it was destroyed by invaders. Today, only ruins remain of these once elaborate structures. The Zimbabwe Empire lasted until the 19th century. The Africans living in this region are so respectful of their ancestors and the magnificent structures they created that when they gained their independence in 1980, they named their country Zimbabwe.

Name: _____ Date: _____

Knowledge Check

Matching

_____ 1. Sahara Desert

_____ 2. Kush Civilization

_____ 3. Ghana

_____ 4. caravan

_____ 5. Mali

_____ 6. Zimbabwe

_____ 7. Great Zimbabwe

a. African city enclosed by a huge stone wall

b. a string of pack animals or wagons that traders used to transport goods

c. the kingdom that included and expanded on the area once controlled by Ghana

d. great desert that covers most of northern Africa

e. empire between the Zambezi and Limpopo Rivers; means "great stone houses"

f. West African empire bordered by the Senegal and Niger Rivers, the Sahara Desert, and jungle

g. old civilization just south of Egypt along the Nile River

Multiple Choice

8. The Kush defeated what other nation and ruled as their kings for about a century?

    a. Egypt

    c. Ghana

    b. Mali

    d. Zimbabwe

9. Ghana was a center for making and trading weapons made of what metal?

    a. gold

    c. iron

    b. bronze

    d. copper

10. Of what were the walls of Great Zimbabwe made?

    a. mud bricks

    c. cement

    b. wood

    d. granite bricks

11. What was an important item at this time, highly prized for its ability to preserve food?

    a. gold

    c. ivory

    b. salt

    d. sugar

Constructed Response

12. How did Ghana become a rich and powerful kingdom? Use details from the reading selection to help support your answer.

_____

_____

_____

_____

_____

Name: _____ Date: _____

Map Follow-Up

There have been many changes to the nations of Africa throughout its history. Some of them have occurred within the past few years. Identify and label each modern African country on the map of Africa below.

Africa

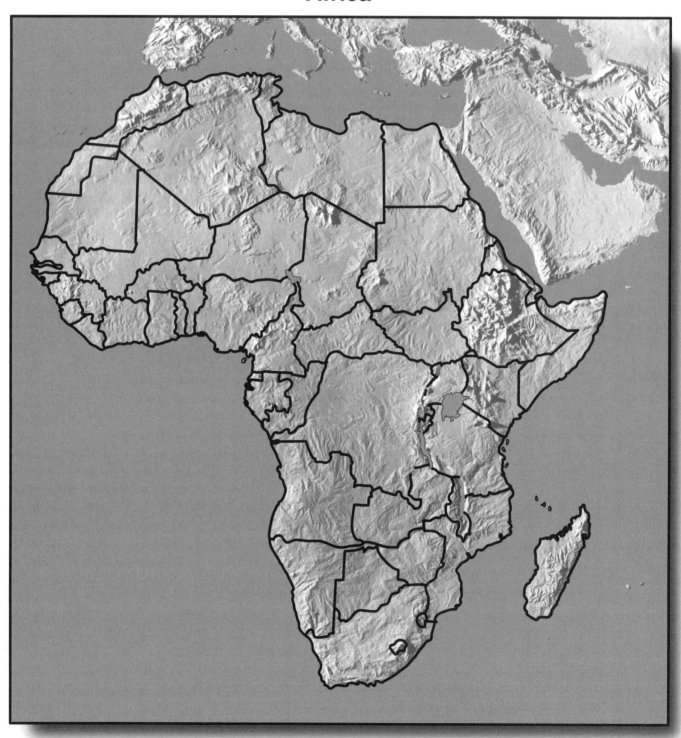

The Americas: The Olmecs

Giant carved stone heads are ruins of the Olmec civilization.

Early People in the Americas

The people we call Native Americans arrived in North America over 20,000 years ago. It took many centuries for these people to populate North and South America. The area between North and South America is called **Central America**. The northern part of Central America, which includes the central and southern parts of Mexico, Guatemala, Belize, western Honduras, and El Salvador, is known as **Mesoamerica**.

The Spanish Conquistadors, who explored Central and South America, discovered highly developed civilizations. These civilizations were similar. Many built pyramids, developed a hieroglyphic type of writing, and created accurate calendars. They were excellent mathematicians and astronomers. They had similar religions and gods. Many also practiced human sacrifice. Four major cultures from Mesoamerica and South America were the Olmecs, Mayas, Aztecs, and Incas.

The Olmecs

One of the first civilizations in Mesoamerica was called the **Olmec Civilization**. In Mesoamerica, there is a wide variety of altitudes, rainfalls, and climates. Some areas are so **arid** they are described as deserts; others are so **lush** and receive so much precipitation they can be called rain forests. It was within this diverse area that the Olmec Civilization had its origin.

Olmecs Discover Corn

The Olmec civilization developed around 1200 B.C. along the southern Gulf coast of Mexico and began with the discovery of how to grow maize. **Maize** is the native word for corn. It was an agricultural society that gradually evolved as a number of small settlements, each built around an Olmec temple. These grew into cities, and over time, the Olmec Culture dominated the Mexican lowland. The civilization lasted until about 100 B.C., when it dissolved for some unknown reason. The influence of the Olmec civilization reached from the Gulf coast to the central highlands in Mexico and southeast along the Pacific coast to El Salvador.

Olmec Temples and Stone Heads

The Olmecs were very religious. They built large temples, monuments, and pyramids to honor their gods and leaders. The Olmecs were noted for the huge carved **stone heads** they made. Two things make these carved stone heads remarkable. First, the Olmecs were a stone-age people, so carving the stone heads must have been very difficult with only stone tools. Second, since no Native American culture used the wheel for transportation, how they transported these 40-ton carvings is a mystery.

Olmec Achievements

Other Olmec achievements include stone pavements, drainage systems, a counting system, and the first calendar in the Americas. Their greatest achievement, though, may well be the influence they had on later civilizations. Many Mesoamerican civilizations can be traced to the Olmec.

OLMEC CIVILIZATION AT A GLANCE

WHERE: Southern Gulf coast of Mexico; influence reached from the Mexican highlands, along the Pacific coast to El Salvador

WHEN: 1200 B.C.–100 B.C.

ACHIEVEMENTS:
- Built temples, monuments, and pyramids
- Developed first calendar in the Americas
- Carved huge stone heads
- Built stone pavements and drainage systems
- Had a counting system
- Influenced later civilizations

Name: _____ Date: _____

Knowledge Check

Matching

_____ 1. Central America

_____ 2. Mesoamerica

_____ 3. Olmec Civilization

_____ 4. arid

_____ 5. lush

_____ 6. maize

_____ 7. stone heads

a. full of green, growing plants

b. the native word for corn

c. dry and desert-like

d. the area between North and South America

e. one of the first civilizations in Mesoamerica that started in about 1200 B.C. along the southern Gulf coast of Mexico

f. huge round carved sculptures made by the Olmecs

g. the northern part of Central America, which includes central and southern Mexico, Guatemala, Belize, western Honduras, and El Salvador

Multiple Choice

8. What was one thing the early American civilizations did NOT have in common?

   a. pyramids

   b. wheeled carts

   c. calendars

   d. astronomers

9. What did the Olmecs use to create the carved stone heads?

   a. wooden tools

   b. metal tools

   c. stone tools

   d. glass tools

10. The Olmecs lived in a specific region known as

    a. Mesoamerica.

    b. Central America.

    c. North America.

    d. South America.

Constructed Response

11. Why was the discovery of how to grow maize important for the development of the Olmec Civilization? Use details from the reading selection to help support your answer.

_____

_____

_____

_____

_____

_____

_____

The Mayas

The Mayas built observatories in many of their cities to aid in their study of astronomy. This observatory in Chichén Itzá still stands today.

One of the most highly developed of the early civilizations in Mesoamerica was the Mayas. The **Mayan Civilization** was located east of the Olmec Civilization in the tropical rain forest in the Yucatán, Guatemala, and western Honduras. It lasted from 1000 B.C. until A.D. 900 and reached its peak about A.D. 300. Most of the Mayas were farmers who grew cotton, corn, and squash and lived in small villages. They built large ceremonial centers with palaces and large pyramids.

Writing, Mathematics, and Astronomy

The Mayas were an intelligent people who developed a complex **hieroglyphic** writing system. They also created an advanced system of mathematics that many feel was superior to that of the Europeans. They were able to accurately predict **solar eclipses**. They also gained an advanced understanding of astronomy from studying the stars, planets, sun, and moon. With their knowledge of astronomy and mathematics, they were able to develop a **solar calendar** that had 365 days. The Mayan calendar was more accurate than the Gregorian calendar developed in Europe in 1582. The Mayas used their solar calendar to plant and harvest their crops. They also developed a second 260-day calendar to mark their religious ceremonies.

Mayan Pyramids

The Mayas were also artists who created sculptures, pottery, monuments, and buildings. The most impressive of their structures were the pyramids, many of which still stand today. The pyramids were 200 feet high and made of stone blocks joined with mortar made of lime. Mayan pyramids were primarily temples. They often had a base of rubble and were sometimes enlarged at a later date. If you were to take a Mayan pyramid apart, you might find several smaller pyramids inside. The Mayan understanding of astronomy enabled the Mayas to build their pyramids with the bases facing north and south. The exterior of Mayan pyramids had staircases that began at the base and rose to the temple chamber at the top.

Ball Courts

Mayan buildings were not restricted to temples and pyramids. They also built **ball courts** in every large city. Young Mayas, covered with padding, used these courts to play a game with a rubber ball. This was a ceremonial game and was not unique to the Mayas. Other civilizations in Mesoamerica and South America also played the same game on similar courts.

Mayas Abandon Their Cities

It is unclear what caused the Mayan civilization to end in A.D. 900. The people appear to have just left their villages. Buildings under construction were left unfinished. For whatever reason, their cities and palaces were abandoned, and the rain forest swallowed what was left of this once magnificent civilization.

MAYAN EMPIRE AT A GLANCE

WHERE: In the Yucatán, Guatemala, and western Honduras

WHEN: 1000 B.C.–A.D. 900

ACHIEVEMENTS:
- Created many sculptures, paintings, and carvings of stone, jade, and turquoise
- Built huge pyramids
- Developed a complex hieroglyphic writing system
- Developed a system of mathematics
- Had an advanced understanding of astronomy
- Developed a 365-day solar calendar

Name: _____ Date: _____

Knowledge Check

Matching

_____ 1. Mayan Civilization

_____ 2. hieroglyphic

_____ 3. solar eclipse

_____ 4. solar calendar

_____ 5. ball court

a. area where Mayas wearing padding played a game with a rubber ball

b. when the sun's light is blocked by the moon and a shadow falls on Earth

c. writing system where pictures stand for words

d. located in the tropical rain forest in the Yucatán, Guatemala, and western Honduras; at its peak about A.D. 300

e. 365-day year; based on the movement of the earth around the sun

Multiple Choice

6. What crop was NOT grown by Mayan farmers?

   a. squash

   c. cotton

   b. corn

   d. wheat

7. The Mayas' 260-day calendar was used for what?

   a. farming

   c. predicting eclipses

   b. planning religious ceremonies

   d. building pyramids

8. What was on the top of Mayan pyramids?

   a. temple chamber

   c. rubble

   b. tomb

   d. palace

9. Who probably played on the Mayan ball courts?

   a. old men

   c. young men

   b. children

   d. women

Constructed Response

10. Describe how the Mayan pyramids were constructed and what they looked like. Use details from the reading selection to help support your answer.

_____

_____

_____

_____

_____

_____

Name: _____ Date: _____

Explore: Creating Hieroglyphics

The Mayas, Egyptians, and other ancient cultures drew pictures to represent ideas or numbers. The pictures they drew are called **pictographs** or **pictograms**. The writing systems they developed based on these pictures are called **hieroglyphics**. Hieroglyphic writing combines symbols that represent ideas, syllables, and sounds into glyphs. These glyphs were used to keep records, transact business, and record history.

Since drawing detailed pictures takes time, writers or **scribes**, as they were called in some cultures, would speed up the process of writing by eliminating some of the details of the glyphs. This process continued so that over a period of time, the glyph became a few simple lines, and it was hard to determine what the original glyph or picture looked like.

Here is an example of how a glyph began as a picture and was simplified into cursive forms over time. The example was created for this exercise only and cannot be found in ancient Mayan, Egyptian, or other hieroglyphic writing. Here is the way the glyph for hunting *might* have been created.

ORIGINAL GLYPH FOR HUNTING   **STYLIZED GLYPH FOR HUNTING**   **FINAL CURSIVE FOR HUNTING**

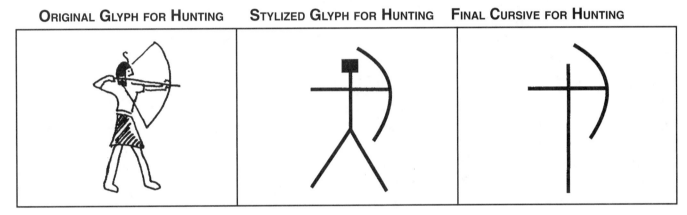

Now it is your turn to create a glyph.
1. Choose an object, event, or an action that is important in your life.
2. Draw a picture of this object, event, or action, and place it under the phrase, "Original Glyph."
3. Draw a stylized picture of the glyph leaving out some of the details, and place it under the phrase, "Stylized Glyph."
4. Draw an abstract version of the glyph with just a few lines, and place it under the phrase, "Final Cursive."

ORIGINAL GLYPH   **STYLIZED GLYPH**   **FINAL CURSIVE**

The Aztecs

The **Aztecs** originally were a small, nomadic tribe in Mesoamerica. The Aztecs had come from the north and spent several years wandering around the Mexican Valley. Sometime during the 13th century they stopped their wandering and settled on the border of Lake Texcoco. They drained swamps and built artificial islands to make gardens. They founded the town of **Tenochtitlán**, which is now Mexico City.

Expanding the Aztec Empire

During the 15th century, the Aztecs expanded their empire by conquering several tribes to the south and extending their boundaries across Mesoamerica. When the Aztecs conquered a tribe, they did not burn their villages or try to destroy the tribe as other empires often did. They made them part of the Aztec Empire. However, those who were conquered by the Aztecs had to pay them **tribute** in the form of food, precious metals,

The Sun god Tonatiuh is carved in the center of the Aztec calendar stone. Others carvings represent the Aztec days and religious symbols.

jewels, textiles, pottery, decorative feathers, cocoa, rubber, and other items to support the Aztec priests and rulers of Tenochtitlán.

Human Sacrifice

The conquered tribes also had to provide victims for **human sacrifice**. Like other Meso-american cultures, the Aztecs sacrificed humans to please the gods. It is estimated that 20 to 50 thousand people were sacrificed each year. Many were slaves or war prisoners. Sometimes, Aztecs were used. It was considered an honor to be chosen to be sacrificed, and the victim felt that he or she would be granted eternal life in return. The sacrificial ceremony was performed by priests at altars on top of layered pyramids. Great crowds would gather to watch the ceremony.

Aztec Crafts and Knowledge

The Aztecs borrowed a great deal from the Mayas and other cultures. Parts of their religion, scientific achievements, calendar, building style, irrigation, astronomy, mathematics, the arts, sculpture, and weaving can all be traced to earlier civilizations. While the Aztecs had the wheel, they did not use it to make vehicles. They used copper and bronze for tools but not iron or steel. Their artisans made beautiful jewelry from gold, silver, and from their alloys, but they did not have glass, plows, gunpowder, or alphabetic writing. They kept written records of their history, religious practices, and other administrative information of their empire in books called *codexes* or *codices*, made of tree bark or leaves. Their writing was a kind of hieroglyphic.

The Aztecs created art and architecture that were very complex and sophisticated. They were also efficient farmers who used irrigation, terracing, and fertilization in their fields. When the Spanish arrived in the 16th century, Tenochtitlán, the administrative and religious capital of the Aztec Empire, was an impressive city.

> **AZTEC EMPIRE AT A GLANCE**
> **WHERE:** Mesoamerica
> **WHEN:** A.D. 1200–1521
> **ACHIEVEMENTS:**
> - Created art and architecture
> - Efficient farmers who used irrigation, terracing, and fertilization
> - Schooling and training in martial arts was compulsory for boys
> - A centralized government controlled every aspect of the Aztecs' lives

The Spanish Arrive and Conquer

It was the arrival of the Spanish that brought an end to the Aztec Empire. Christopher Columbus reached the Caribbean in 1492. This gave the Spanish a base in Cuba and other islands. Other Spaniards, called **conquistadors**, came to Mexico. The conquistadors continued their exploration in search of gold, land, and people to convert to Christianity. One of the Spanish conquistadors was **Hernando Cortés**.

Cortés landed on the Yucatán Peninsula in 1519 with 600 men. This was a small force, not nearly as many as the Aztecs had. However, as Cortés marched toward Tenochtitlán looking for gold, natives who had been conquered by the Aztecs joined him. These natives hated the Aztecs and wanted to be free of their domination. Cortés was able to get over 150,000 natives to join him.

When Cortés and his army arrived in Tenochtitlán, the Aztecs were cautious but welcomed them. The Aztec emperor, **Montezuma II**, gave them gold and other valuable gifts. Cortés took Montezuma hostage anyway. Montezuma was killed, supposedly by the Aztecs, and the Spanish attacked Tenochtitlán. Cortés' huge army, armed with gunpowder, armor, and horses, was too much for the Aztecs, but they continued to resist. Then Tenochtitlán became infected with smallpox, and the **epidemic** wiped out half of the city. Cortés seized Tenochtitlán in 1521. Within five years, Cortés had conquered all of the Aztec territories. The Aztec civilization was over. The Spanish destroyed much of Tenochtitlán and put up many new buildings. They changed the name of Tenochtitlán to Mexico City. Spanish rule soon spread throughout the newly conquered land.

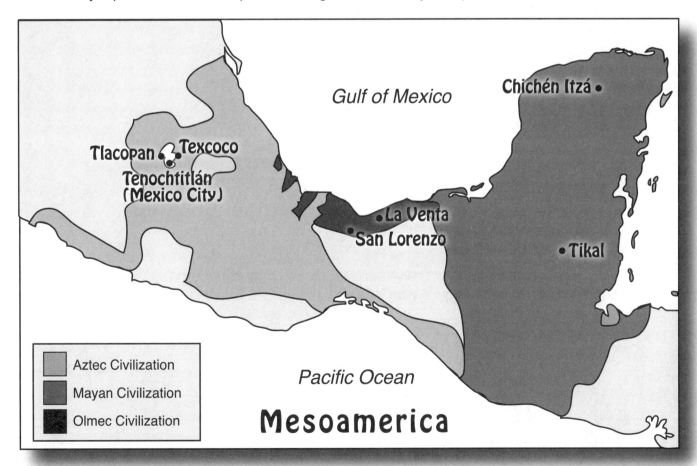

Name: _____ Date: _____

Knowledge Check

Matching

_____ 1. Aztecs

_____ 2. Tenochtitlán

_____ 3. tribute

_____ 4. human sacrifice

_____ 5. codexes

_____ 6. conquistadors

_____ 7. epidemic

a. nomadic tribe from northern Mexico who wandered around the Mexican Valley and finally settled on Lake Texcoco

b. Aztec books made out of tree bark or leaves

c. items the conquered tribes had to pay to the Aztecs

d. a sudden, widespread outbreak of deadly disease

e. the Aztecs' capital city; now the location of Mexico City

f. killing people in religious ceremonies to please the gods

g. Spanish soldiers who conquered the native people of the Americas

Multiple Choice

8. Where did the Aztecs plant gardens?

    a. on artificial islands

    b. on the tops of mountains

    c. in their backyards

    d. in open fields

9. How many people may have been sacrificed each year by the Aztecs?

    a. 200–300

    b. 2,000–5,000

    c. 8,000–10,000

    d. 20,000–50,000

10. What material did the Aztecs NOT have?

    a. gold

    b. glass

    c. bronze

    d. silver

11. What disease brought by the Spanish wiped out half of the Aztecs in Tenochtitlán?

    a. influenza

    b. chicken pox

    c. measles

    d. smallpox

Constructed Response

12. Why did the Aztecs not destroy the villages and tribes they conquered? Use details from the reading selection to help support your answer.

_____

_____

_____

_____

_____

_____

_____

The Incas

While the Aztecs and other civilizations were thriving in Mesoamerica, a unique civilization was developing in the Andes Mountains in South America. It was the largest civilization during this period, and its population was about twice that of England. This was the **Inca civilization**, and it lasted from about A.D. 1400 to 1532.

Incan Temple of the Sun in Ingapirca, Ecuador

Origins of the Incas

The origins of the Inca civilization are not clear. The Incas had no written language, so what we know about their history is based on what the Incas told the Spanish conquistadors. Some of this may have been a mixture of fantasy and legend. It is likely that the beginnings of the Inca civilization were in about 1100 when a small tribe settled in the Cuzco Valley in the Andes Mountains of South America. They spoke a language called **Quechua**. In their language, they used the word *Inca* to refer to their rulers. Today, **Inca** refers to their civilization. For many years, the Incan culture was very similar to other cultures in the area. They had a strong state with the city of **Cuzco** as its capital. However, in the late 1300s, the Incan Empire, under the leadership of Pachacuti, began to expand from the Cuzco region of the Andes Mountains.

Expanding the Empire

Pachacuti Inca Yupanqui was an excellent ruler and military leader. While he reorganized the government and rebuilt the capital, he began to attack and defeat nearby tribes. The battles of conquest were brutal invasions, and resistance was crushed. Some tribes realized they were not strong enough to defeat the Incas, so they joined them and fought on their side. Soon, the Incan army was so large that most tribes offered little resistance. As the empire grew, the Incas built roads and established military strongholds in order to maintain their newly gained territory.

After about ten years, Pachacuti's son, Topa Inca Yupanqui, took over the army and continued the Incan expansion. Under Topa Yupanqui's leadership, the Incan Empire expanded along the western coast of South America and even into the rain forests. The Incas required those who were conquered to accept the Incan culture. They had to learn the Quechua language and worship the Incan gods, and they were subject to the Incan laws. In order for the conquered people to learn the Incan culture, the Incas supplied teachers to instruct them in such things as how to grow crops and how to build villages the Inca way. Those who would not comply either became slaves or were sent somewhere else to live. The land of those who were banished was given to those who accepted the Incan culture.

Incan metalwork

Ruling the Empire

The Incas did not directly rule the conquered tribes. They would let local rulers retain their positions if they were loyal to the Incas and if they fought on their side. Each tribe was independent and was ruled by a council of elders. The tribe was loyal to the ruler of the empire who was called the "Inca." They believed he was descended from the sun god. While

---

INCA EMPIRE AT A GLANCE

WHERE: The Andes Mountains of South America

WHEN: A.D. 1100–1532

ACHIEVEMENTS:
- Created beautiful art
- Developed a method of counting and record keeping by using a process of tying knots in strings
- Great advances in medicine
- Built a large network of stone roads
- Expert builders who cut stones by hand and built structures without mortar

---

the conquered tribe became an Incan tribe, they still maintained local control. The Incan Empire was more like a group of independent tribes that shared the same culture.

Incan Medicine

Some of the most notable achievements of the Incas were in the field of medicine. While the Incan view of disease could be called primitive, their treatments were remarkably effective. They believed that sickness was either a punishment from the gods or the result of evil magic. When someone was sick, the first treatment was to make a sacrifice to please the gods. They also used amulets, spells, and chants to rid the patient of evil. This often worked. We know today that a patient's confidence in his doctor and his treatment are very important in recovery.

The Incas used herbs to treat many diseases, such as dysentery and ulcers. One of the medicines, **quinine**, which the Incas used to cure fever, is used today in the treatment of malaria and heart irregularities.

The Incas performed many medical feats that were remarkable for their time. Surgeon-priests performed brain surgery and amputated limbs when needed. Prior to the surgery, the surgeons would have patients chew coca leaves in order to dull the pain. **Coca** is a shrub native to South America. After the surgery, the surgeon would burn or cauterize the wound to deaden the feelings and prevent infection. Then they would bite off the heads of large ants and use the jaws of the ants to clamp the wound shut. Surgeon-priests also performed blood transfusions hundreds of years before scientists in other parts of the world did. Since many Incas shared the same blood group, these transfusions were usually successful.

The Spanish Arrive

In the early part of the 16th century (1500s), when the Incan Empire was at its height, Spaniards started exploring the Americas. **Francisco Pizarro**, a wealthy Spaniard living in Panama, had heard of how Hernando Cortés had conquered the Aztecs in 1521. Pizarro also wanted to gain more wealth and fame. He had heard of a rich empire that existed on the coast of South America. When King Charles V of Spain appointed Pizarro the governor of Peru, he took about 200 soldiers into the Andes Mountains searching for this wealthy civilization. He found the Incan Empire in turmoil. Over 250,000 Incas had died of smallpox, a disease unknown in their land before Europeans had arrived. There had also been a civil war between two brothers, Huascar and Atahualpa, who fought to become the ruler of the Incan Empire. Atahualpa had won, but the empire had been weakened.

In 1532, Pizarro marched into the Incan city called Cajamara and met with **Atahualpa**, the new Incan leader. Since there were so few Spanish and so many Incas, Atahualpa felt he had nothing to fear. When he arrived, however, Pizarro's men attacked and massacred the Incas. This was easy to do since the Incas were unarmed, and Pizarro had cannons, muskets, steel swords and spears, and soldiers on horseback. With Atahualpa as a hostage, the Spaniards were able to loot the Incan camp.

The End of the Incan Empire

Atahualpa offered to buy his freedom with a room full of gold. Pizarro agreed, but after the ransom arrived, Pizarro broke his promise. He put the Incan ruler on trial. Atahualpa was charged with killing his brother, worshipping idols, and having several wives. Atahualpa was found guilty and was executed. Without a leader, the Incas were unable to organize well enough to defend themselves. Pizarro was eventually able to conquer the Incas.

Atahualpa paid a huge ransom, but the Spanish executed him anyway.

Name: _____ Date: _____

Knowledge Check

Matching

_____ 1. Inca Civilization
_____ 2. Quechua
_____ 3. Inca
_____ 4. Cuzco
_____ 5. quinine
_____ 6. coca
_____ 7. Francisco Pizarro
_____ 8. Atahualpa

a. a medicine the Incas used to cure fever
b. the word used to refer to the Incan ruler
c. the last Incan ruler, who was executed by the Spanish
d. leaves of this shrub helped dull pain
e. people who lived in the Andes Mountains of South America, with a population twice that of England
f. the capital of the Incan Empire
g. the language of the Incas
h. leader of the Spanish expedition that conquered the Incas

Multiple Choice

9. What had weakened the Incan Empire shortly before the Spanish arrived? (Circle any that apply.)
   a. civil war
   b. earthquake
   c. crop failure
   d. smallpox

10. Which Incan ruler was the first to greatly expand the empire?
    a. Atahualpa
    b. Pachacuti Inca Yupanqui
    c. Topa Inca Yupanqui
    d. Huascar

11. How did Incan surgeons close wounds?
    a. with stitches
    b. with glue
    c. with wooden pins
    d. with ant jaws

Constructed Response

12. How were conquered people treated by the Incas? Use details from the reading selection to help support your answer.

_____
_____
_____
_____
_____
_____
_____

Name: _____ Date: _____

Explore: Piecing Together an Artifact

1. Divide your students into five groups.

2. Cut the graphic shown below along the dotted lines and give each group one of the pieces. Make sure that the groups can't show their fragments to the other groups.

3. Explain that they are to assume they are archaeologists and have just discovered a fragment of a sculpture. Based on that one fragment, they are to decide what the original, whole sculpture looked like.

4. Give the individual groups time to discuss what the original sculpture looked like. Then have each group draw a picture of the original sculpture based on their discussion. Collect the pictures.

5. Have each group join another group and have them piece their two fragments together. Then have them repeat the process they have just gone through. Again, have them draw another picture based on their discussion. If a group that has a fragment of the top part of the sculpture joins with one that has a fragment of the bottom part of the sculpture, their resulting picture should be similar to the original. If groups that both have either top parts or bottom parts merge, their resulting picture will probably be quite different. You may want to repeat Step 5 with three groups to see if the pictures become even more accurate.

6. Share each of the five first pictures with the class. Which is the most accurate? Share the second pictures with the class. Which are the most accurate? Share the third pictures, if the groups completed a third round of pictures. Which are the most accurate? Discuss the problems they had in completing the assignment and relate them to the problems that archaeologists have in working with artifacts.

Glossary

acropolis – a high place or hill in a Greek city; often a sacred place where temples were built

agora – the marketplace of a Greek city

agriculture – farming; growing crops and raising livestock

Akkad – country of the Akkadians where the Tigris and Euphrates Rivers are close together

Akkadians – group of Semitic people who moved into Sumeria from the Arabian Peninsula

Alexander – rose to power in Macedonia at age 20 and conquered the Persians, Egyptians, and parts of Iran and the Indus Valley; called Alexander the Great

alphabet – a writing system where each symbol stands for a sound in speech

Anatolia – the ancient name for Asia Minor; known as Turkey today

Arabs – people who live in Arabia

arid – dry and desert-like

aristocracy – rule by a ruling class of people; often nobles or landowners

Aryans – what the Persians called themselves

Asgard – the home of the Viking or Norse gods

Ashur – original capital of the Assyrian civilization

assembly – a governing body in Athens consisting of all citizens

Assyria – a civilization in Mesopotamia on the upper Tigris River; greatest between 1600 and 612 B.C.

astrology – the belief that the positions and movements of the stars and planets can affect or predict life on Earth

astronomy – the study of the universe, including the movement of the stars and planets

Atahualpa – the last Incan ruler, who was executed by the Spanish

Athenians – people from Athens

Attic Peninsula – peninsula on the southeast coast of Greece where Athens was located

Augustus – title that meant "great"; what Octavian was called after assuming power as the first emperor of the Roman Empire

Avesta – the Persian holy book, based on the views of Zoroaster

Aztecs – nomadic tribe from northern Mexico who wandered around the Mexican valley and finally settled on Lake Texcoco

Babylonia – kingdom that covered all of Mesopotamia, ruled by King Hammurabi

ball court – area where Mayas and other native civilizations played similar types of games with a rubber ball

barbarians – invaders who lived outside the Roman Empire

berserker – a brave Viking warrior who wore a bear skin and worked himself into a frenzy to prepare for a fight

Bible – the Christian holy book; contains the Old Testament, which tells the history of the Hebrews, and the New Testament, which tells of the life of Jesus Christ and his disciples

Black Land – what the Egyptians called their country, referring to its fertile soil

Bosporus – a narrow strait of water between Europe and Asia

bull-jumping – grabbing a bull by the horns, flipping over it, and landing on one's feet on the ground

Byzantine Empire – another name for the Greek Eastern Empire; named after Byzantium, the former name of Constantinople

Byzantium – the first name of the capital of the Byzantine Empire; also the name of the culture of this Empire

caliphs – rulers of the Muslim Empire

caravan – a string of pack animals or wagons that traders used to transport goods

Carthage – the most famous Phoenician trading post; located in northern Africa

Celts – people of Indo-European stock who first appeared in Central Europe and moved into Western Europe and the British Isles

Central America – the area between North and South America

Christianity – religion developed by the followers of Jesus Christ

citizen-soldier – a soldier who returns home and resumes his life when the fighting is over

civilization – a high level of cultural and technological development, especially when systems of writing and record keeping have been created

Classical Period – time in Greek history from about 800 to 323 B.C.; also called the Golden Age of Greece

coca – leaves of this shrub native to South America were used by the Incas to dull pain

Code of Hammurabi – a set of laws and punishments developed by the king of Babylonia

codexes or **codices** – Aztec books made out of tree bark or leaves

comedies – plays designed to be humorous or to poke fun at certain people or situations

communal – shared or used in common by a group or members of a community

compensate – pay back an equal amount for an injury or loss

Confuciansim – religion that developed from the philosophy of Confucius

Confucius – philosopher and teacher who lived in China from 551 B.C. to 479 B.C.; taught politeness, sincerity, unselfishness, respect for laws, and hard work

conquistadors – Spanish soldiers who conquered the native people of the Americas

Constantine the Great – Roman emperor who rebuilt Byzantium as the capital of the eastern part of the Roman Empire; renamed the city Constantinople

Constantinople – name of the capital city of the Greek Eastern Empire; previously Byzantium; named after the Roman Emperor Constantine the Great

consuls – two men given authority to make decisions for the Roman Republic

cuneiform – writing consisting of shapes and lines produced by using a wedge-shaped instrument on a clay tablet

Cuzco – the capital of the Incan Empire

Cyrus the Great – ruler of a Persian province who defeated the Medes and united the Medes and Persians into a strong army and conquered almost all of the ancient world

Dark Ages – another name for the Middle Period in Greek history when culture declined

Delian League – group of Greek city-states united with Athens to provide money for a stronger army to defeat the Persians; later started attacking other city-states

Delta Region – the area of the Nile River where silt is deposited before the water empties into the Mediterranean Sea

democracy – rule by all the people being governed

dictator – someone the Roman senate appointed to deal with a crisis

drama – telling stories through acting and dialog

Druids – the priests or learned class of the Celts; served as teachers, judges, and doctors

dynasty – a series of rulers from the same family or line

Early Period – time in Greek history when the Minoan and Mycenaean Civilizations flourished; from before 2000 B.C. to about 1200 B.C.

emperor – the ruler of an empire

engineer – a person who uses science, math, and planning to design and build things that are useful for others

epic poem – long poem that tells a story

epidemic – a sudden, widespread outbreak of deadly disease

Etruria – region in central Italy where the Etruscans lived

Etruscans – ancient people who lived in central Itay and were in power from about 800 to 300 B.C.

Exodus – the Hebrews' escape from Egypt; means "to leave"

exported – sent out of the country

Fertile Crescent – an arch-shaped area in the Middle East from the Persian Gulf through the Tigris and Euphrates River Valleys and along the Mediterranean Sea

fortified – protected by huge stone walls

Francisco Pizarro – leader of the Spanish expedition that conquered the Incas

Gate of Ishtar – the most impressive opening in the wall around Babylon; named in honor of the goddess Ishtar; made of colorful glazed enamel bricks with pictures of animals

Genghis Khan – name that means "mighty lord"; leader of the Mongols

Ghana – West African empire bordered by the Senegal and Niger Rivers, the Sahara Desert, and jungle

granary – a place to store grain

Great Pyramid of Giza – the largest pyramid built by the Egyptians; honors the pharaoh Khufu or Cheops; one of the Seven Wonders of the Ancient World

Great Wall of China – built to keep out invaders; built over a period of 2,000 years; over 4,500 miles at its longest

Great Zimbabwe – African city enclosed by a huge stone wall

Greek colonies – outposts set up by Alexander and run by his soldiers in the countries he had defeated

Greek Eastern Empire – the eastern half of the Roman Empire governed from Constantinople

Hagia Sophia – church built in Constantinople in 532–537; today it is a Muslim mosque

Hanging Gardens of Babylon – building with irrigated terraces planted with trees and flowers and having pools and fountains; one of the Seven Wonders of the Ancient World

Harappa – one of the centers of the Indus Valley Civilization; rediscovered in 1921; located near the head of the Indus River

Harappan Culture – another name for the Indus Valley Civilization; named for the city of Harappa

Hattusa – the capital of the Hittite Kingdom

Hebrews – a nomadic group of Semitic people who settled near the Mediterranean Sea; ancestors of today's Jews

Hernando Cortés – the leader of the Spanish soldiers who conquered the Aztecs

hieroglyphics – a writing system where pictures stand for words

Hippocratic Oath – deals with ethics in medicine; doctors still promise to follow its principles

Hittites – migrant peasants who lived north of the Black Sea and then moved into Anatolia

Homer – blind Greek poet who lived in about 800 B.C. and wrote epic poems about Mycenaean heroes

horoscope – a prediction of a person's future based on a diagram of the stars and planets at a given moment

hospital – a place to care for those who could not care for themselves

Huang He – river that flows from the Tibetan Highlands across China to the Yellow Sea; also called the Yellow River

human sacrifice – killing people in religious ceremonies to please the gods

Hyksos – invaders from Canaan who had superior bronze weapons and horse-drawn chariots; they conquered the Egyptians in about 1800 B.C.

Iliad – the story of the war between Greece and Troy; epic poem written by Homer

imported – brought into the country

Inca – the word the Incas used to refer to their ruler; also used today as the name of the civilization

Inca Civilization – people who lived in the Andes Mountains of South America from about A.D. 1400 to 1532, with a population twice that of England at the time

Indus Valley – region in what is now Pakistan and western India, along the Indus River

Indus Valley Civilization – the people who lived along the Indus River and developed one of the world's first great urban civilizations

iron – a strong metal that can be extracted from certain kinds of rocks and made into tools and building materials

Islam – religion founded by Muhammad; means "surrender to the will of Allah"; the Muslim religion

Israel – what the Hebrews called the area in the Mediterranean where they settled; the name of the modern Jewish state in the Middle East

Istanbul – name given to the capital city of the Ottoman Turks; previously Constantinople and Byzantium

jarls – Viking aristocrats or nobles

Jerusalem – the Hebrews' capital city

jihad – a holy war waged by Muslims, such as the Ottomans

Judaism – the Jewish religion

Julian calendar – calendar created by Sosigenes in 46 B.C. at the request of Julius Caesar; based on the solar year, each year had 365 days and 6 hours divided into 12 months

Julius Caesar – a Roman general and hero who became dictator in 46 B.C. and was assassinated on March 15, 44 B.C.

karls – Viking freemen; free-born peasants

88

keystone – a wedge-shaped stone in an arch that causes the arch to lock together

Knossos – the main city of Crete that had a huge palace

Kush Civilization – old civilization just south of Egypt along the Nile River

Lao-tzu – Chinese philosopher living about the same time as Confucius; taught people to live very simple lives in harmony with nature, be happy with what you have, and sit quietly and meditate

Latin Western Empire – the western half of the Roman Empire governed from Rome

leisure time – time to spend on activities not directly related to survival

letters – the basics of Greek education; reading, writing, and arithmetic

longships – Viking fighting ships up to 90 feet long and holding 50 warriors

Lower Egypt – kingdom located in the northern part of Egypt

lucomon – a priest-king who ruled an Etruscan city-state; selected from the nobility of the city

lush – full of green, growing plants

Macedonia – rugged, mountainous area north of Greece; its people were considered barbarians by the Greeks

maize – the native word for corn

Mali – the kingdom that included and expanded on the area once controlled by Ghana

Mayan Civilization – located in the tropical rain forest in the Yucatán, Guatemala, and western Honduras; at its peak about A.D. 300

Medes – warriors who raided cities and caravans and settled in the same area as the Persians

mercenary – a foreign soldier hired by another country to fight in its army

Mesoamerica – the northern part of Central America, which includes central and southern Mexico, Guatemala, Belize, western Honduras, and El Salvador

Mesopotamia – the land between the Tigris and Euphrates Rivers; from the Greek word that means "between two rivers"

metallurgy – the science and technology of metals

Middle Kingdom – the second period of the Egyptian Civilization; from 2040 to about 1800 B.C.

Middle Period – time in Greece from about 1100 to 800 B.C.; also called the Dark Ages; culture declined during this time

Ming Dynasty – Chinese dynasty that lasted from A.D. 1368 to 1644; the great wall began to be reconstructed in stone during this dynasty

Minoan Civilization – the first civilization in Europe; on the island of Crete and other islands in the Aegean Sea; named after their king Minos

Mitanni Kingdom – introduced trained horses and chariots to the Mesopotamian region

Mohenjo-daro – one of the centers of the Indus Valley Civilization; located about 350 miles downstream from Harappa along the Indus River

monarch – a ruler, such as a king

monasteries – places where religious men called monks lived and worked

Mongols – one of the nomadic tribes of the Asian steppe who united under Genghis Khan to become a nation of fierce warriors and conquer the largest empire in world history

monotheism – believing in only one god

Montezuma II – the last Aztec emperor; taken hostage by Cortés and killed during fighting between the Aztecs and the Spanish

Moses – a Hebrew who had lived as an Egyptian for part of his life; got the Israelites released from bondage in Egypt and led them out of Egypt and on a journey through the wilderness

mosque – a place where Muslims worship

Muhammad – a prophet who founded the religion called Islam in Arabia

mummification – the process of preserving a dead body by drying it

Muslim Empire – empire begun under the leadership of Muhammad, which took over parts of the Persian and Byzantine Empires, and by the eighth century extended from Spain to India

Muslims – people who practice the Islamic religion

Mycenae – the best-known city of the Mycenaean Civilization

Mycenaeans – people who arrived on the mainland of Greece about 2000 B.C. and became dominant about 1450 B.C.

mythology – a collection of myths used to explain customs, ways of life, or aspects of the natural world

myths – stories about the Greek gods; any stories created by different cultures to explain how things on Earth came to be

New Kingdom – the third period of the Egyptian Civilization; from about 1600 to 1100 B.C.

Nile River – flows from Lake Victoria in present-day Uganda and north through Egypt to the Mediterranean Sea

Nineveh – later capital of the Assyrian civilization

nomadic – moving from place to place with no permanent home

nomarchs – governors of different sections of Egypt

Odyssey – the story of a Mycenaean soldier's journey home after the Trojan War; epic poem written by Homer

Old Kingdom – first period of the Egyptian Civilization; from 3100 to 2040 B.C.

oligachy – rule by only a few people; often the wealthiest people

Olmec Civilization – one of the first civilizations in Mesoamerica that started in about 1200 B.C. along the southern Gulf coast of Mexico

Olympic Games – athletic contests started in Greece in 776 B.C. to honor the god Zeus

orally – through the spoken word; by word of mouth

Ottoman Empire – named after the leader Osman I, and eventually included the areas of the old Seljuk states, the Byzantine Empire, the Balkans, southern Russia, and northern Africa

papyrus – paper-like material made from reeds

patricians – the wealthy class in Rome

Peloponnesian League – group of small city-states joined with Sparta to oppose the Delian League

Peloponnesian Peninsula – peninsula in southern Greece where Sparta was located

Peloponnesian War – war between Athens and her allies (the Delian League) and Sparta and her allies (the Peloponnesian League) 431–404 B.C.

Persian Empire – located east of the Fertile Crescent on the east side of the Persian Gulf in what is now Iran and Afghanistan

pharaoh – the king or ruler of Egypt

Philip II – the king of Macedonia and Alexander the Great's father

Phoenicians – traders and seafaring people who lived along the Mediterranean coast in what is now Lebanon

phoinikes – Greek word meaning "purple men"; where the name Phoenician comes from

pictographs – pictures that stand for words

plebeians – the common people of Rome

polis – an independent Greek city-state

polytheism – believing in many gods

province – new land acquired by the Romans

Punic Wars – three wars between Rome and Carthage over a hundred-year period

quartz – a six-sided crystalline mineral that may be present in the sand used to produce glass

Quechua – the language of the Incas

quinine – a medicine the Incas used to cure fever

Red Land – what the Egyptians called the desert surrounding their country

Remus – one of the twin brothers who founded Rome; supposedly nursed by a wolf; killed by his brother Romulus

republic – a political system in which a group of citizens elects representatives and officers to run the government

Romulus – one of the twin brothers who founded Rome; supposedly nursed by a wolf; killed his brother Remus to become the first king of Rome

sagas – stories of Viking adventures

Sahara Desert – great desert that covers most of northern Africa

satrap – a governor of a Persian province

satrapies – the 20 provinces into which Darius divided the Persian empire

Scandinavian – from the countries of Norway, Denmark, and Sweden; also Finland and Iceland in modern times

scribes – professional writers

Seljuk Turks – people who conquered most of the Near East part of the Muslim Empire and were eventually defeated by the Mongols

Semitic – the language family that includes Hebrew, Aramaic, and Arabic

senate – the assembly of aristocrats who elected or appointed people to perform public jobs in the Roman Republic

Shang Dynasty – period in China when cities were planned and people were divided into social ranks; from about 1766 B.C. to 1122 B.C.

Shang Ti – the most important Chinese god; "the Ruler Above"

Shi Huang Ti – the first emperor of China

silk – a very thin cloth made from cocoons spun by silkworms; the main export of China

Silk Roads – trade routes from China to West Asia and Europe

silt – rich soil deposited by a river

smelting – the process of extracting metal from ore

social equality – when all people in a society are treated the same

solar calendar – 365-day year; based on the movement of the earth around the sun

solar eclipse – when the sun's light is blocked by the moon and a shadow falls on Earth

Spartans – people from Sparta

Sphinx – huge stone sculpture of a creature with the face of a human and the body of a lion; built in Giza near the Great Pyramid

standing army – composed of soldiers who choose the army as a career; when they are not fighting, they are training

steppe – harsh grassland between Siberia and northwest China; Slavic word meaning "grassland"

stone heads – huge, 40-ton, round carved sculptures in the shapes of heads made by the Olmecs

strategy – careful plan for how to fight a battle or deal with an enemy

stylus – a wedge-shaped instrument used for writing on clay tablets

sultan – Turkish word for the emperor of the Ottoman Empire

Sumer – the country of the Sumerians on the Plain of Shinar near the Persian Gulf

Sumerians – the first group to inhabit Mesopotamia; lived in the Plain of Shinar near the Persian Gulf; the first to invent a written language and the wheel

Taoism – philosophy developed by Lao-tzu; from tao, which means "way"

Temujin – the name Genghis Khan was given at birth

Tenochtitlán – the Aztecs' capital city; now the location of Mexico City

Thebes – defeated Sparta in 371 B.C. and ruled Greece for a few years

things – open-air meetings all freemen could attend to discuss problems and settle disputes

thralls – slaves in Viking society; prisoners of war or children whose parents were thralls

Torah – the Jewish scriptures

trade – exchanging goods or services with other people

tragedies – serious plays telling of a conflict between the main character and some superior force where the ending is usually sad or disastrous

tribunes – representatives of the common people in the Roman senate

tribute – payment that conquered people were required to pay the conquerors

Tuscany – modern region of Italy from the Tiber River to the Arno River where the Etruscans once lived

Upper Egypt – kingdom located in the southern part of Egypt

Valhalla – a hall in Asgard where dead warriors were brought back to life; considered a paradise where those who died in battle would enjoy themselves by fighting and feasting

Vikings – from a word that means "pirates"; Norsemen who came from Scandinavia and were feared as fierce raiders

Xia (Hsia) Dynasty – the first dynasty of kings to rule China; from about 2205 to 1766 B.C.

ziggurat – a temple-tower that was the center of a Sumerian city

Zimbabwe – empire between the Zambezi and Limpopo Rivers; means "great stone houses"

Zoroaster – a Persian prophet who had seven visions

Zoroastrianism – religion founded by Zoroaster based on his seven visions

Answer Keys

The Fertile Crescent: Knowledge Check (p. 3)
Matching
1. c   2. b   3. e   4. a
5. d
Multiple Choice
6. b   7. c   8. a   9. c
Constructed Response
10. The people in the Fertile Crescent began to trade excess crops and animals with others. They needed to develop a written language to keep records. They developed laws, mathematics, agriculture, and medicine. The population grew, and they had to find ways to live close to one another.
Map Follow-Up (p. 4)
Teacher check map. Countries are: Egypt, Israel, Lebanon, Jordan, Saudi Arabia, Syria, Turkey, Iraq, Kuwait, and Iran

Mesopotamia: Knowledge Check (p. 7)
Matching
1. d   2. h   3. g   4. a
5. c   6. f   7. b   8. e
Multiple Choice
9. b   10. a   11. d
Constructed Response
12. There was fertile soil in the area around and between the Tigris and Euphrates Rivers. They could grow many different crops. However, they had to learn to build levees and irrigation canals to control the flooding rivers and deal with the hot, dry climate. They could use mud from the rivers for building material. The biggest disadvantage was that the land did not provide any natural protection from invaders. Enemies could attack from any direction.

Babylonia: Knowledge Check (p. 10)
Matching
1. f   2. e   3. c   4. a
5. b   6. d   7. g
Multiple Choice
8. a   9. c
Constructed Response
10. The Code was trying to give appropriate punishments for each

crime, instead of sentencing people to death for even minor crimes. "An eye for an eye, and a tooth for a tooth" meant that an equal punishment would be given. The Code also had different levels of punishment depending on the social class of the person wronged.

The Assyrians: Knowledge Check (p. 12)
Matching
1. d   2. c   3. b   4. e
5. a
Multiple Choice
6. d   7. b   8. a
Constructed Response
9. The Assyrians were on the upper Tigris River. They did not have to irrigate like in Babylonia. The land received water from the river and from rainfall. There were rocks and stones available for building in Assyria. The disadvantage of Assyria was that the land was harder to cultivate, and they were often attacked by barbarians.

The Hittites: Knowledge Check (p. 14)
Matching
1. c   2. a   3. e   4. f
5. b   6. d
Multiple Choice
7. c   8. b   9. d
Constructed Response
10. The Hittite law tried to compensate the person who was wronged. The person who committed the crime would have to pay a fine to the person he injured. This way the injured person received justice and the wrongdoer was not given an extreme punishment.

Ancient Egypt: Knowledge Check (p. 16)
Matching
1. f   2. c   3. d   4. a
5. e   6. g   7. b
Multiple Choice
8. d   9. b   10. a

Constructed Response
11. The Egyptians believed in life after death. A person's soul would continue to live as long as the body was preserved. They came up with mummification as a way to preserve the body for as long as possible.

Egypt's Three Kingdoms: Knowledge Check (p. 19)
Matching
1. e   2. c   3. a   4. f
5. b   6. g   7. d
Multiple Choice
8. b   9. c   10. a
Constructed Response
11. The Pharaoh Menes assigned nomarchs to govern different parts of the kingdom. To communicate with the nomarchs, the Egyptians developed a written language called hieroglyphics. They also created a paper-like material from papyrus reed on which to write. Then the nomarchs gained power and some broke away to establish their own provinces. This broke Egypt into two separate kingdoms for a time.

China: Knowledge Check (p. 22)
Matching
1. a   2. c   3. e   4. f
5. b   6. h   7. g   8. d
Multiple Choice
9. c   10. b   11. a
Constructed Response
12. The ancient Chinese believed that when a person died, he or she went to live with Shang Ti. Their dead ancestors then had powers to help them make wise decisions or to punish them. So they wanted to keep their ancestors happy. They worshipped them, built temples for them, and held many celebrations to honor their ancestors.

The Mongols: Knowledge Check (p. 26)
Matching
1. d   2. f   3. e   4. a
5. c   6. b

Multiple Choice
7. d   8. a   9. c
Constructed Response
10. The Mongol Empire became the largest empire the world has ever known. The grandsons of Genghis Khan conquered most of Asia and parts of Europe. The empire covered an area that included the countries that today are known as Mongolia, China, Korea, Russia, India, much of the Middle East, parts of Europe, and all the area in between.

The Indus Valley: Knowledge Check (p. 28)
Matching
1. c   2. d   3. b   4. f
5. a   6. e
Multiple Choice
7. c   8. b   9. a   10. d
Constructed Response
11. The buildings and streets were neatly arranged according to a grid system. Each city had a large granary and water tank. Homes were made of bricks and plaster. The houses were large with several rooms that led to a courtyard. Some homes had wells for drinking water and bathing, bathrooms with toilets, and a system for drainage. Mohanjo-daro had drainage and sewage systems for the city.

The Minoans: Knowledge Check (p. 31)
Matching
1. e   2. c   3. a   4. g
5. b   6. f   7. d
Multiple Choice
8. b   9. d   10. a
Constructed Response
11. People had leisure time to devote to activities not directly related to survival. Some people were free to create art, fashion jewelry, and make items that people used. Others became merchants trading food and other items. This trade led to even more wealth for the Minoans. There was social equality since everyone could af-

ford to live well. Sports and other activities developed. Boxing and bull-jumping were popular.

The Mycenaeans: Knowledge Check (p. 33)
Matching
1. a   2. e   3. d   4. g
5. b   6. f   7. c
Multiple Choice
8. a   9. b   10. d
Critical Thinking
11. Answers may vary, but may include: The stories were told from generation to generation before they were finally written down by Homer. Each time the stories were told, they added or changed things to make them more interesting and heroic.

Explore: Greek Word Roots (p. 34)
1. DRAMA   2. ODYSSEY
3. SCHOOL   4. SPARTAN
5. GYMNASIUM
6. ANCHOR   7. COMEDY
8. TRAGEDY   9. POET
10. MATHEMATICS
11. PHILOSOPHY
12. TYRANT   13. MONARCH
14. BIOLOGY   15. ORCHESTRA
16. THESPIAN 17. ECOLOGY
18. HERO   19. POLITICS
20. GEOMETRY
21. GRAMMAR
22. DEMOCRACY
23. DICTATOR 24. ANTISEPTIC
25. CHURCH   26. EPISODE

Athens and Sparta: Knowledge Check (p. 37)
Matching
1. f   2. e   3. d   4. g
5. b   6. a   7. c
Multiple Choice
8. c   9. b   10. b
Constructed Response
11. At one time, the Greeks had leaders similar to kings. Then the landowners became the ruling class and established an aristocracy. This was replaced by an oligarchy where only a few people ruled. These were the wealthiest people in the town. Some Greek

city-states such as Athens established a democracy. All citizens were able to vote and decide how to run the city-state. Sparta was ruled by two kings and a council.

The Golden Age of Greece: Knowledge Check (p. 40)
Matching
1. d   2. g   3. e   4. c
5. a   6. f   7. b
Multiple Choice
8. b, d   9. a   10. b   11. d
Constructed Response
12. The government in Athens was a democracy. All citizens were members of the governing body called the assembly. A citizen was a free man who was born to Athenian parents. The assembly met every nine days to make decisions on laws, buildings, and other matters. Each citizen could vote on matters in the assembly. He also had the right to speak at the assembly in order to influence others.

Alexander the Great: Knowledge Check (p. 44)
Matching
1. e   2. b   3. a   4. d
5. c
Multiple Choice
6. d   7. a   8. b   9. c
Constructed Response
10. As he conquered more territory, Alexander set up Greek colonies in these lands. They were run by his soldiers. This brought the Greek language and culture to those areas. The Greeks were the main influence in these lands for several hundred years after Alexander's death.

Map Follow-Up (p. 45)
In any order: Greece, Macedonia, Albania, Montenegro, Serbia, Bulgaria, Turkey, Armenia, Azerbaijan, Syria, Lebanon, Israel, Jordan, Egypt, Saudi Arabia, Iraq, Kuwait, Iran, Afghanistan, Turkmenistan, Uzbekistan, Tajikistan, Pakistan, India

The Etruscans: Knowledge Check (p. 47)
Matching
1. d   2. a   3. e   4. b
5. c   6. f
Multiple Choice
7. b   8. a   9. c
Constructed Response
10. The Etruscans had no strong central government. There were a number of city-states. They formed a league of 12 cities. Each city was ruled by a priest-king called a lucomon. The lucomon was elected each year from the nobility that governed each city.

The Celts: Knowledge Check (p. 49)
Matching
1. b   2. c   3. e   4. a
5. d
Multiple Choice
6. d   7. a   8. b   9. b
Constructed Response
10. The Celts had no written language. Their history and literature was memorized and passed down orally from generation to generation. The Druids preserved this knowledge and served as teachers, judges, and doctors.

Ancient Rome: Knowledge Check (p. 53)
Matching
1. d   2. h   3. c   4. e
5. f   6. b   7. i   8. g
9. a
Multiple Choice
10. a   11. d   12. c
Constructed Response
13. Each new land acquired by the Romans became a province. The Romans signed a treaty with each defeated nation requiring them to pay taxes to Rome. The important people of the conquered nation could become Roman citizens, vote in elections, and become elected to public office. If they became Roman citizens, they had to adopt a Roman name and wear Roman clothes. Even those who didn't become citizens often adopted the Roman language and customs.

Explore: The Julian Calendar (p. 54)
1. November   2. October
3. February   4. December
5. August   6. June
7. March   8. July
9. January   10. September
11. May   12. April

The Vikings: Knowledge Check (p. 57)
Matching
1. d   2. h   3. a   4. g
5. c   6. e   7. b   8. f
Multiple Choice
9. c   10. b   11. a
Constructed Response
12. A region's wealth was often stored in the monastery. They planned their raids for Sunday when they knew the people and monks would be in church. They could sail their longships in close, raid the monastery, put the loot and kidnapped monks on the ship, and escape before the people could mount an organized defense. They could sell the monks as slaves in the East.

The Phoenicians: Knowledge Check (p. 59)
Matching
1. e   2. c   3. b   4. a
5. d   6. f
Multiple Choice
7. c   8. a   9. b   10. c
Constructed Response
11. The Phoenicians developed their sailing skills by sailing all over the Mediterranean world, looking for new markets and raw materials for their products. They may have sailed around Africa. They were among the first people to learn to sail at night by navigating by the stars.

The Hebrews: Knowledge Check (p. 61)
Matching
1. d   2. f   3. a   4. c
5. g   6. e   7. h   8. b
Multiple Choice
9. c, d   10. b   11. d

Critical Thinking
12. Answer may vary, but might include: When a king or group of nobles made a set of laws for governing the common people, they often did not obey the laws. The Hebrew laws based on religion applied to everyone, including the rulers. The laws were part of their religion and everyone had to follow them.

The Persians: Knowledge Check (p. 63)
Matching
1. e   2. b   3. d   4. a
5. g   6. c   7. f
Multiple Choice
8. a   9. b   10. d
Constructed Response
11. The Babylonians were unhappy with their own king. They knew the Persians would treat them fairly. They would be allowed to keep their own culture if they paid tribute to the Persians. They would get a better ruler and a better-run government with the Persians.
Map Follow-Up (p. 64)

Ruling such a large empire required a good administrator and organizer. Darius divided the empire into 20 satrapies, each managed by a satrap. This made it easier to govern the empire. An inspector would visit the satrapies unannounced to make sure the satraps were doing their jobs. The Persians built well-paved roads to make it easier to connect the empire and encourage trade.

The Byzantine Empire: Knowledge Check (p. 67)
Matching
1. g   2. c   3. f   4. a
5. e   6. b   7. d

Multiple Choice
8. b   9. a   10. c

Constructed Response
11. Byzantium was a valuable port that was on both sides of the Bosporus. This was a narrow strait of water between Asia and Europe. This was the sea route that connected the Black Sea and the Mediterranean Sea. Trade between Europe and the East went through the route. Also, armies marching from west to east or east to west tended to pass through this area. It was conquered by many different groups over the years.

The Muslim and Ottoman Empires: Knowledge Check (p. 69)
Matching
1. i   2. d   3. h   4. g
5. e   6. a   7. c   8. f
9. b

Multiple Choice
10. c   11. b

Constructed Response
12. During the reign of Suleiman the Magnificent from 1520 to 1566, the Ottoman Empire reached its greatest power. The Ottomans conquered the Balkans, southern Russia, and northern Africa. The empire included much of eastern Europe and western Asia. Suleiman had mosques, monuments, bridges, roads, and schools built. He encouraged the arts and sciences.

Explore: Three World Religions (p. 70)
1. I   2. J   3. J, C, I
4. I   5. I   6. C   7. J
8. C   9. C   10. J   11. I
12. C   13. J   14. I   15. C
16. J   17. J   18. I   19. C
20. J   21. C   22. I   23. C
24. I   25. J, C, I

Africa: Kush, Ghana, and Zimbabwe: Knowledge Check (p. 73)
Matching
1. d   2. g   3. f   4. b
5. c   6. e   7. a

Multiple Choice
8. a   9. c   10. d   11. b

Constructed Response
12. Ghana's location allowed it to become rich and powerful. It controlled the roads and charged taxes on caravans passing through the kingdom. It controlled the trade of gold, iron, and salt. Ghana was the center of the iron industry.

Map Follow-Up (p. 74)
Teacher check map.

The Olmecs: Knowledge Check (p. 76)
Matching
1. d   2. g   3. e   4. c
5. a   6. b   7. f

Multiple Choice
8. b   9. c   10. a

Constructed Response
11. The discovery of how to grow maize led to the development of an agricultural society. Since they could grow crops, they didn't have to wander around in search of food. They settled in small villages built around a temple. These small settlements grew into cities, and the Olmecs dominated the Mexican lowlands.

The Mayas: Knowledge Check (p. 78)
Matching
1. d   2. c   3. b   4. e
5. a

Multiple Choice
6. d   7. b   8. a   9. c

Constructed Response
10. The Mayan pyramids were 200 feet high and made of stone blocks joined with mortar made of lime. They often had a base made of rubble. They were sometimes enlarged at a later date. Smaller pyramids were covered with larger pyramids. The bases faced north and south. There were exterior staircases that began at the base and rose to the temple chamber at the top.

The Aztecs: Knowledge Check (p. 82)
Matching
1. a   2. e   3. c   4. f
5. b   6. g   7. d

Multiple Choice
8. a   9. d   10. b   11. d

Constructed Response
12. The Aztecs made the conquered villages part of the Aztec Empire. Then the villagers had to pay tribute to the Aztecs. This included food, precious metals, jewels, textiles, pottery, decorative feathers, cocoa, and rubber. They also had to provide victims for human sacrifices.

The Incas: Knowledge Check (p. 85)
Matching
1. e   2. g   3. b   4. f
5. a   6. d   7. h   8. c

Multiple Choice
9. a, d   10. b   11. d

Constructed Response
12. The Incas let local rulers retain their positions if they were loyal to the Incas and if they fought on their side. Each tribe was independent and was ruled by a council of elders. The tribe was loyal to the emperor, called the "Inca." Conquered tribes maintained local control. The Incan Empire was more like a group of independent tribes that shared the same culture.

94